"A masterful debut in devastatingly beautiful prose about disquieting things. She lays bare the dark hearts of our sentimentalized HDB 'Heartlanders' and our vaunted government 'scholars' and finds: coldness, sanctimony, and corrosive attitudes the more damaging for their utter casualness. This is a passionate warning, a chronicle of tragedy foretold. How will we save our selves and our soul? Like Anthony Chen's film *Ilo Ilo*, *A Certain Exposure* already has the feel of an essential Singapore classic."

**—Sandi Tan, author of *The Black Isle***

"An intimately layered story about twin brothers forging different paths through the intricacies and prejudices of Singapore society, but will strike a chord wherever the struggle between personal values and social pressures is experienced."

**—Ovidia Yu, author of *Aunty Lee's Delights***

# A Certain Exposure

## Jolene Tan

A novel

EPIGRAM BOOKS / SINGAPORE

Copyright © 2014 by Jolene Tan

Lyrics to "I Could Be Dreaming" are copyright © 1999
by Jeepster Recordings and published by Sony/ATV Music,
and are used by permission only.

Author photo copyright © 2014 by Dan Yeo for White Room Studio

All rights reserved
Published in Singapore by Epigram Books
www.epigrambooks.sg

Edited by Jason Erik Lundberg
Cover design and layout by Lydia Wong

National Library Board,
Singapore Cataloguing-in-Publication Data

Tan, Jolene, 1982–
A certain exposure / Jolene Tan. –
Singapore : Epigram Books, 2014.
p. cm
ISBN: 978-981-07-8828-5 (paperback)
ISBN: 978-981-07-8829-2 (ebook)
1. Twins – Fiction.
2. Hope – Fiction.
3. Betrayal – Fiction. I. Title.

PR9570.S53
S823 -- dc23    OCN869720778

This is a work of fiction. Names, characters, places,
and incidents either are the product of the author's imagination
or are used fictitiously. Any resemblance to actual persons,
living or dead, events, or locales is entirely coincidental.

First Edition: April 2014

10   9   8   7   6   5   4   3   2   1

*For Mark and Pei Chi—the core team*

"It's not a terrible thing—I mean, it may be terrible, but it's not damaging, it's not poisoning, to do without something one wants […] what's terrible is to pretend that the second-rate is first-rate."
—Doris Lessing, *The Golden Notebook*

"A family's like a loaded gun:
You point it in the wrong direction,
Someone's gonna get killed."
—Belle and Sebastian, "I Could Be Dreaming"

"Old bureaucrat, my comrade,
it is not you who are to blame."
—Antoine de Saint-Exupéry, *Wind, Sand and Stars*

# MARCH 1998

Brian organised for the body to be flown back. His parents had been stoic enough for every other administrative task, but not for this. For a while they considered having Andrew cremated in Britain, returning, like so many dregs of tea, in a pot. But Brian could not bear the idea that he might not see Andrew again—the real Andrew, not just bits and flakes produced from his oxidisation at high temperatures. So he stepped up to the job, to phone calls with Human Remains in the airline's cargo department, to have his brother's corpse sent home.

Now, in the void deck, peering uncertainly, Brian wasn't sure why it had been important. A pot of ashes might have been preferable for not pretending to any likeness. His expectation that the thing in the casket would be Andrew had ebbed away. In his mind his brother was browned, lithesome, handsome; and though there are good reasons to doubt an identical twin's assessment on those points, everyone else, too, found the head framed in the pearly padded lining remote and undersized, the skin false, almost papery. Not for the first time, "Human Remains" struck

Brian as inapt, even cruel. The human was gone.

He moved onto a chair. These were laid out in rows, bright red plastic under the white lights that hurt his eyes. He had the uneasy and unreasonable feeling that he hadn't looked for whatever vague duration might count as enough. His mother stood by the casket, her arms pressed tightly across her lower ribs, her face smudged with fatigue. His father a few seats away, looking at nothing in particular. Together they formed a loose-jointed triangle of mourners.

The sketchy theory occurred to Brian that he should move to console his parents. But the Hollywood-toned images he conjured felt hollow. An arm around a shoulder? They were not a family who touched. A sympathetic phrase? They were literal, practical people, speaking where it was useful, not given to sharing emotions. And what good could such a discussion do? Grief, guilt, anger, despair, blank exhaustion, even a kind of irritableness—as seemed so often the case, it must be impossible, Brian thought, that verbalising any of the things he felt could give comfort.

As a child, like many children, Brian had been afraid of his parents dying. This expressed itself not in subjective feelings of fear—he would not have used the word "scared"—but in a masochistic, periodically recurring obsession. Nine years old, perched on a kitchen stool, he stared at his mother as she scraped at the bottom of the rice cooker, her profile silhouetted against the bright patches of tree showing between diagonal window grilles. You'll go, you'll go. You're here now, but you won't be. You'll go. Across the table, oblivious, Andrew hunched over a book of brain teasers. When he looked up, Brian froze, averted his eyes, began to regard his cutlery intensely and without seeing. His heart pounded. You'll go. You'll go. The large rice bowl chinked solidly on the table and his mother took her place at the corner.

"Brian, dinner."

"Yes, Mum."

He would close the car door behind him and become immediately certain that his father was pulling off into a collision, a delivery van perhaps, or, swerving to avoid a jaywalker, a bus. He pulsed with momentary hatred of the hypothetical pedestrian. This was more than a decade before the Nicoll Highway collapsed. His imagination did not extend to the spontaneous crumbling of tonnes of concrete.

In his teens he sometimes approached the ultimate taboo, allowing himself to think the word *cancer*, but in a disciplined, sidelong way, never front and centre. His images of that eventuality were always rigorously vague. Once his parents took a flight without the boys, a short trip to Hong Kong, and he drove himself into an ecstasy of panic until they called from Kai Tak with a reminder not to let strangers into the flat. After that he subsided into a few days of blithe ordinariness. At one point, in a darkened cinema, he even focused single-mindedly on the question of how to hold hands with Cherilyn from Bukit Panjang Girls' School. But then he remembered, stiffening with horror at his own neglect: his parents were scheduled to be midair at that very second. They might even have sunk, glassy-eyed, half an hour earlier, beneath the foamy waters of the South China Sea.

It was entirely superstitious. Pure childishness. Not the fears, which were reasonable, and as these things go, indeed realistic: but the dutiful, limpet-like attention to these scenarios, the ritual invocations, the sense that his anticipation was a kind of magic charm. It was always the thing taken for granted that the universe snatched away, wasn't it? If he stayed on the ball, his visions were forbidden, by some hazy but compelling, almost mathematical, certainty from materialising. More pragmatically—a relative description— if he kept himself conscious of their mortality, he could never be reproached for undervaluing their presence when they did eventually go.

Brian knew, quite simply, that he *needed* his parents; he avoided thinking about whether he *liked* them. There were punishments reserved for such ingratitude.

He'd never imagined Andrew dying, of course. Andrew was a grubby, competitive presence, crowding the womb, wailing snottily from fifteen minutes prior to Brian's infancy, and then hanging about, unavoidable, for the rest of it: like a law of nature or a reflection in the mirror. When you share a bed with your older brother, and he snores, and kicks you in the shin in the middle of the night, you shove him away and think with irritation and envy of prosaic possibilities, like one day having your own room.

Now, when it was arguably most pertinent—when Andrew had actually died—Brian was reluctant to picture his final moments. Maybe "reluctant" was the wrong word: he was simply not moved to do it. The frenetic energies invested so involuntarily and so persistently in visualising so many other fatal sequences had, here, faltered.

The foreignness of it all was against him. He could recite easily enough the bare, infamous facts of the situation, but they were strings of words, opaque to him. Pictures Andrew had shown him of Corpus Christi College in Cambridge University were dominated by smiling undergraduates. He had at most only background glimpses of the place itself: of curt, clipped circles of grass; darkened dining halls; sandy walls of stone. English air in March, winter and its end, were theories only: neither fresh cold nor dry electric heat came within his experience. He had never seen a photograph of Andrew's room—or had he? He had after all seen, well, that picture. But it revealed little of the room, if that was indeed where it had been taken, to say nothing of the window. Curtains (what patterns?) or blinds? What was the view—cobblestone street, closed square college courtyard, temperate tree? (Themselves all further mysteries.) And what colour were the bedsheets Andrew had looped around his neck and tied to the window handle, cutting his blood flow and killing his brain—so said the doctors—just before dawn?

It was hopeless. Nothing could be made of the material. And if Andrew was so partially imagined in life, it seemed to Brian grotesque to fill in the blanks in death.

This went too for the biggest blank of all. There was no suicide note. Speculation was inevitable, and repulsive. My brother killed himself because. Because of a photograph, because of a prank, because of malice, because of his nature, because of a panic, because of a misunderstanding (on his part, on everyone else's), because of all of the above, because of none of the above. My brother killed himself because. Brian would not fill in the blank. My brother killed himself.

# JUNE 1987

OUTSIDE, THE RAIN unrolled in fat grey sheets, palpating walls and windows with a steady thrum, punctuated with intermittent deep-chested rumbles. The storm-time air was cool: the earth's usual cloak of humidity had lifted. The floor's tiles were luxuriously cold against Brian's knees and thighs and elbows and belly.

He had begun reading out of boredom. What he had really wanted to do was look for Priya. The book she had sparkled over seemed the next best thing, like he was learning something about her, a one-way conversation at least. He slid quickly in—it was ease and brilliance. When he surfaced, just before Chapter Eleven, the sturdy fall of water had given way to the filliping rat-tat of the roof run-off and to the emergent whirr of the ceiling fan. He sat up, stretched and considered.

He wanted to *know*. What would happen when they met the King? Their three-bedroom flat in this Braddell estate could not produce wonders to match these vain sorcerers and falling stars. Priya might not be there today. It would be wet. On the other hand (he stirred), the spell was already broken (he was on his feet). Something had uncoiled in his legs; his thigh and shoulder muscles were firing urgent little twitches. The air was still enticingly fresh. He had to be moving. It was an occupational hazard of being twelve years old.

He went into his bedroom to shelve the book. Andrew was asleep, peacefully enough. There had been a lot of muttering and jerking the night before. Their cousin Mabel, whose mother was their mother's sister, sat at their desk with the inevitable Bible, a chunky volume she toted almost everywhere. Brian found it vaguely sinister, partly because it was Mabel's, and partly because it seemed, from the one time he had looked inside, deathly boring. The text was tiny and drab. Someone "begat" (what?) someone who lived for some implausible length of time and then "begat" someone else of someplace, bizarre names no one in real life would have. (The same could be said of his beloved fantasy novels, but those were not laid out, like a fossil record, with this tone of laboured verisimilitude.) On request Mabel showed him the bit about Noah and the ark, which he recalled from a picture book somewhere, but it was lifeless—no giraffes, no vigour in the waters.

It made him suspicious that the writing was not just difficult but unreachably distant, relying on retelling for charm or on translation for meaning. To hear Mabel speak, it was not a book at all, as he knew them, but a decoder-passport to shadowy authorities, to peculiar (and burdensome) commitments. Like roleplay games but in earnest, or like school but weirder. This was, to him, wholly unlike real reading and its real pleasures—the pleasure of the enchanted castle which wanders fields—where the unusual or unknown pivots suddenly into total and private view. Brian's love of stories did not survive adolescence, but at twelve they ruled him, they had set him standards, and the Holy Bible did not make the cut.

Though they tried to be discreet, his parents, too, viewed Mabel's Christianity with reservations. Her mother, Poh Lian, had begun to attend church after marrying a fairly nominal believer. This was the immediate source of Mabel's affection (as Brian's parents saw it), and that was innocent enough, but they had misgivings about its ultimate origins. Christianity was the ang moh religion, a supercilious British import. Lim Poh Ling and Teo Kim Seng made poor cultural purists: they spoke English at home and at work, they had bent with the winds to give their sons "high class" ang moh names, and they plied the boys with ang moh books to improve their exam results. But that was practical. This was different, this ang moh God, this Jesus Christ. (The Trinity escaped them, but they saw these two as collapsible.) It was, well, it was weird.

This was no battle of faiths. Whatever the government census claimed in its eagerness to classify, their attachment to Buddhism was so slender as to seem, if you looked from the side, to be hardly there at all. It was the very notion of devotion, of worship, of purity, of doctrine and abstract morality, that bothered them. Particularly worrying were tales, transmitted in scandalised whispers, of converted children who refused to attend funeral ceremonies on the most abstruse grounds. Superstition, they called the traditional rites for paying respect to the dead. Devil worship. "Who is this ang moh, this Jesus Christ, so important ah, more important than her Ah Kong? Her Ah Kong leh, her Ah Kong you know!" Christianity caused weird behaviour which flew in the face of both economic gain and social ease, rather like the stories they used to hear, in lower whispers still, of people who had given away all their money, and thrown aside comfortable lives in Singapore, to serve the revolution in the motherland. Christianity and Communism were body-snatchers. And so, oddly enough, Brian's aesthetic objections and his parents' unimaginative ones converged.

Nevertheless, Mabel had volunteered to come each day and watch over Andrew while he sweated and moaned his way through the fever; and Brian's parents were impressed and grateful. Mabel was not Brian's favourite person, but if she hadn't been there, he would probably have spent the start of the long school holidays sitting by Andrew himself, so he was grudgingly glad of her presence after all.

"I'm going out," he said.

"Where?"

Like she needed to know. "Downstairs lorh."

"Don't come back late ah. And don't mix with gangsters."

"Yah lah." The enduring mystery of Mabel: how could she be in Secondary Two, only fourteen, and already talk like an auntie?

His annoyance fell away quickly, at some point out the door, into his slippers, along the corridor and three flights down. (One up would get him to the lift for his block, but he hadn't yet learned teenage laziness.) Priya wasn't in Frankie Wong Books. He glanced into the bakery next door, scanned the corner coffee shop, and then made for the playground where they had last parted. He had been sitting cross-legged on one tyre swing, suspended from a pyramid of chains; she dismounting from another, dusting gold sand off her shorts and her calves in the slanting evening light. His heart fell: both tyres now hung undisturbed, gleaming wetly. No sign.

He wandered onto the damp sand and stood for a moment. The book again, after all, or the bakery perhaps, and kueh ambon? He had half-turned to go when she called his name, and he looked again at the tiled concrete tower standing in the heart of the playground. She was peeking out from the dingy cavern within, visible only dimly through a small, diamond-shaped hole. (Later, and not very much later at that, he forgot his encounters with Priya Menon almost totally, retaining only the essentials: how she made him feel, what she came to mean. But even so, Brian felt a loss greater than simple nostalgia, as these weathered playground structures in their kingdoms of sand were replaced in almost every housing estate—grey columns, giant birds and stony dragons giving way to open metal frames and plastic squares on rubbery foam.)

He ducked in and joined her in a half-crouch. The space was ringed round with the small diamond windows. A knife-edge of light slid in above the platform, by their heads. They smiled at each other. "I'm reading that book," he said, to be speaking of something. "It's good."

"It is, right? I'm so glad you like it. Have you got to the part where the wizard—oh, I'd better not spoil it for you."

"They're going to the King next. The castle is cool. I like the doors thing, with the colours."

"Yes! I wish I thought of things like that. The walking and the doors and the talking fire. So many cool things together. You know, for composition, I can never think of something new, I always copy. I copied the doors, and from another series, dragons who think in rainbow patterns and you can hear them in your head."

Her ease, her talking, these unfolding packages of thought, amazed him. He had a year's reprieve before the mortifying, ungovernable teenage erections; but every time she said "you", and he watched her looking closely at him, he prickled with aliveness along his haunches and in the small of his back. He was very aware of the length and nearness of her arms, the sand giving slightly under his rubber-slippered feet, the close circling of the walls around.

He felt full of something, he wasn't sure what. Something heavy, glimpsed between sliding panels. It was only as the afternoon drew to a close—after they'd monkeyed about on the climbing frames and the fireman's poles; after Priya's wonder that Brian's brother could and did look *exactly like him* ("I really want to see you together"); after Brian's sympathetic horror at tales of Priya's most imperious classmates ("Mabel my cousin is just like that also")—it was only then, as Brian was taking himself home, across the bare concrete of the void deck and up two steps at a time, that the fullness and the heaviness drained away into a kind of clarity. He was happy.

Between his own unconsciousness and Brian's haze of elsewhere, Andrew saw little of his brother. Eight hours a night they slept side by side. But Brian bounced out of bed early each morning, and when he returned Andrew was usually asleep, exhausted from a day of sweating and headaches and pains behind his eyes.

The dengue was poorly timed. It didn't even bring the compensation of a Medical Certificate to get him out of school. A weekend was all Andrew had of the June holidays before the fever began, and the promised month of freedom opened with a week of fatigue, discomfort, the frustration of time burning away in enforced waste, and Mabel. (Aiyoh, Mabel.) It wasn't a combination he would have chosen for himself.

But Mabel, among these elements, surprised. Perhaps they had always been unjust to her, or perhaps something about his present neediness satisfied her desire for control. Whatever the reason, she was far more tolerable than the shared opinions of the brothers had led him to expect. She sat with her book, and waited, and asked for nothing. As his temperature approached its restless peaks she gently and efficiently applied a damp cloth. In his alert intervals they managed some commonplace exchanges about their family, and exams, and the current Li Nanxing drama serial. And she anticipated his thirst with regular hot mugs of barley, where Brian, he realised, would have had to be asked, before coming in with glasses filled at the kitchen sink.

As he himself would too, Andrew thought, were he nursing anyone: a strange idea to entertain. He propped himself against his pillow and considered Mabel's back as she sat at his desk. She was pencil thin, with a craning pony neck framed by a severe bob. He was for the first time clear-headed enough to appreciate how many hours she was spending in the sole company of a twitching, largely comatose cousin, half a stranger anyway, and to wonder why, exactly, she was there.

"Mabel, you don't find it very boring meh?"

She replied carefully, without turning round: "Find what boring?"

"Sitting here nothing to do, must be very sian, right?"

"I'm studying the Lord's word." This line was a shade more brittle in the air than in her head, where she had practised it enough times, silently, in response to more or less the same question. But she couldn't tell Andrew that, any more than she could tell him the rest, the things she barely acknowledged to herself: that there was nowhere else she had money or permission to go, which would lie beyond the Brownian motion of her mother's rattan and her rage.

"The Lord's word." He couldn't quite keep the laugh out of his voice.

"I know you don't believe in that."

"No, I don't." But it kept Mabel there, with damp cloth and barley. That was something. He had to respect that.

They became friends of a sort. After several days, Andrew's fever subsided. A watch was no longer strictly necessary, but Andrew was still too weak to leave the flat. Mabel continued to come by, and they sat together as they had gotten used to doing. (Brian roamed, and spent the family dinners in distraction. He remained sharp to Mabel, who noticed it for the first time, by contrast with the altered behaviour of his brother.) Andrew immersed himself in mathematical puzzles and a series of faded science books that Mabel fetched from the local library on request. He was particularly preoccupied with one on the human body, full of pictures, the large grey coils of the intestines and the fist-like lump of the heart. Mabel kept to her Bible with the occasional foray into *The Straits Times*. Once or twice they played Uno or Monopoly, and sometimes they watched SBC 8 dramas and afternoon cartoons in companionable silence.

A few days into this routine, Mabel insisted on tuning the television in to an interview. "What is this?" Andrew asked.

"It's one of the people they arrested. For the plot."

He stared blankly.

"Don't you read the news?"

"Er, no."

"So you don't know about the plot?"

"No?" This line of inquiry struck him as unnecessary—she'd been there with him, after all, while he was convalescent for a week.

"These Catholics were arrested, yah, and the government put them in jail. They might be there forever. They don't get to go to court or anything. So they're trapped lah. And this guy, Vincent Cheng, he's one of them, they're letting him out for this interview on TV."

He looked at the screen. A bespectacled, soft-spoken man was being questioned by four journalists. "What were they arrested for?"

Contempt glittered in her voice. "Government says they're dangerous."

"What was their crime?"

"They didn't *do* any crime."

"So how come they were arrested?"

Mabel wouldn't be drawn further: her attention was fixed on the screen. To be sure, Mabel moved in mysterious ways, but still the sight of someone about his age voluntarily paying heed to the news was baffling and impressive. Well, why not, Andrew thought, and settled himself down to watch. He tried to listen as unfamiliar phrases reeled past. Vincent Cheng, in the frame of the box, was asked about, and spoke of, Marxism. A classless society. An open, critical attitude. The ideals of the Church.

Andrew was as ignorant about politics as any twelve-year-old boy. But he was intelligent, and careful, and encouraged to be conscious of his intelligence, to expect high things. He understood his future achievements, unspecified but undoubted, as part of his identity. And if the historical, national and global context of the words he heard passed him by, nevertheless he recognised in them, with sympathetic kinship, a kind of ambition, a kind of identity, thwarted and sidelong.

This kinship frightened him. On the television, Vincent Cheng's face was studiedly blank, his voice dull. He didn't strike Andrew as dangerous or criminal, but as someone hollowed out in defeat. As if his guts were being scraped out with a spoon (he saw the large grey coils), and the air was being pressed out of his lungs (he saw empty, gasping bags), and his innards were now deposited in an ignominious public heap. The result was not an interview but fleshy puppetry, limp and grotesque.

The show ended. Mabel clicked the television off, stood by the set in silence for a moment, and then turned with an air of martyred grandeur.

"Those people who do the Lord's work are always persecuted."

This classically Mabellian sort of line had, in the past, been the subject of a great deal of eye-rolling between Andrew and his brother. Now he felt a kind of sick recognition at its truth. The man on the television had gambled something real and of value in himself, a small feathered thing he should have kept close. If they sensed you were keeping it from them, those who wanted it had jail and journalists and other powers; they could cut you open and scoop it out.

You had to tame it for them. You had to be on their side, the winning side. You had to keep it close.

Andrew made himself a promise. He would never do *the Lord's work*.

Priya Menon, eleven years old, didn't realise just yet how far she was disqualified from social notice, though others regularly did their best to educate her. It would be some time before their efforts bore real fruit, but in the meantime they were disagreeable enough. There was the day, for instance, when Michael Ong of 6A, tittering to himself, sauntered into the prefects' room to claim his school bag. Seeing Priya bent over homework, he came to stand by the table. "Eh, Priya, you always like joking one, right? Here, I tell you this one. What's the difference between an Indian and a bucket of shit?"

She stared into his long, beaming face, oily with the onset of adolescence. His thick hair was stiff with styling mousse. Why would anyone ask this question? Why would *he* ask it? Why would he ask *her?*

"The bucket!" He released a hiccupping laugh. She felt her mouth twist involuntarily. Michael continued, "Eh, don't so serious lah! This one is my sister told me one, quite funny, horh?" She shrank automatically as he reached out to squeeze her upper arm with unexpected force.

Having retrieved his things, he left as suddenly as he had come. Priya willed herself to act as though he had not been there at all. She looked at the next problem sum in her workbook. Her heart was racing. She had to read the words twice before they made sense, and as she wrote in the blank space below, she could see her first equation wobbling. She stopped, looked up for a moment into the silent room, and then went on with grim doggedness. The feel of Michael's fingers stayed with her for the rest of the day, a hot, invisible mark.

Mostly she refused to be rattled. She treated the cries of "Ah pui ah!" and "Fatty bombom!" as cosmic background radiation, and learned to drift quietly into sharp imaginings when her classmates babbled in the impassably alien tones of Mandarin as though she was not there. She decided that the real world consisted of what her cleverness and her sunniness earned her: her parents' love, the praise of her teachers, shared laughter with the scatter of breezy, chatty, good-natured girls at school toward whom she unerringly sailed. The real world was lying across the comforting expanse of her father's stomach, on the sofa, while he hummed to himself and stroked her hair. When Michael thrust his Brylcreemed jibes in her face, or the boy who collided with her in the swimming pool shouted "Mangali cheebye!" she dismissed their abuse as the vaporous excrescences of marginal cranks, like the venomous muttering about *munjen* she heard from her uncle Sundar now and then.

The real world was made up, also, of imaginary ones: books, about tesseracts, ancient artefacts, and dark shadowy powers loosed by arrogant young wizards who had then to pursue them across the sea. Priya couldn't be down about the pale life going on around her when here was such vivid proof of heart-catching beauty, of thrilling fellowships, of vital stuff. She thought everyone would strive for these things—would be pulled, as water ran downhill, toward their deep charm, once they only knew of them. She thought everyone confined to the cardboard day-to-day must feel their own ignorance like an aching hollow. Since fiction and its possibilities were there for the taking, it could only be a matter of time before they learned. Therefore the indignities she endured were evanescent, already scheduled for doom; and so, from her child's-eye view, with all of futurity stretching before it, they were not quite real. Someday soon, her peers would see the light; if not in Primary Six, well, she gave it till Secondary Two at the latest.

When Brian Teo had bumped into her in the book-lined aisles of Frankie Wong, it had all the feeling of a door finally opening from the waiting room into this real world.

"Sorry," he said, retrieving the book he had knocked from her hands and offering it to her with a nervous, solicitous smile.

"It's okay," she said, thinking that he was very handsome. She was slightly surprised to be thinking it. It wasn't something she thought often. When her friends giggled over poster pin-ups or boys at school, she often felt unmoved, and sometimes impatient. Brian had neat features—sharp cheekbones, a clean jaw, lively eyes crinkled at the corners by a ready smile. His face already had a grown-up sort of clarity of expression, not the wet, uncertain look of children; though it would change little through his teenage years, as if it had got ahead early and then stalled.

Priya was drawn to Brian. She didn't want him to go, but she sensed that, left to his own devices, he probably would. "You like fantasy?"

"Yah," he said—not expecting conversation, but clearly not displeased.

"Me too! What are you reading?"

"I just finished *Voyage of the Dawn Treader*, third one in the Narnia series, you know it? I'm looking for number four."

"Reepicheep," she said. "I love Reepicheep! He would be so nice as a pet, right? Just the right size to hug."

Brian smiled. "Yah, but better don't say in front of him, later he stab you, then you know."

"I used to like hiding in cupboards," Priya said. "I liked to jump out and shout 'Boo!' at my mother. But then I read Narnia number one—do you know it?—and then suddenly the cupboard felt too small. Where's the forest? And the talking lion? And don't have any snow."

"Put a lot of moth balls inside lah," Brian suggested. "Can pretend. But might be smelly." They both laughed.

"Number three is the best," she went on. "It's not as good later. Have you read this?" She plucked another volume from the shelf and thrust it at him. "She writes in all this really weird stuff, and at first it seems like it's all anyhow like that, you get confused by it, but then suddenly it all comes together, and it's all *tight*, it all makes sense." This grew into a second recommendation, and then a third. Brian listened with surprised pleasure: it was hard to interest his brother, and the gang at school would enthuse only about battles. A pile of books soon gathered in his arms, but his pocket money only allowed one at a time. "Then you *have* to start with *this one*," she said as they left the store, and he suggested they get some Milo. They sat together on the bright green rail running along the edge of an enormous storm drain, and drank the cold malty chocolate, through straws, out of soft plastic drawstring bags.

That was the first of their handful of June afternoons together. In it Priya learned that Brian lived two blocks away from her; that he attended a nearby Catholic boys' school; that his father worked for the Ministry of Labour and his mother was a police officer; and that he had one brother. A mundane list, not the stuff of adventure or revelation. But she stored these facts up like burnished, hard-edged pebbles, to be turned over and over in her mind that night, while she lay staring at the glow-in-the-dark stars and crescents stuck to the ceiling. They were countable, touchable; they kept the encounter anchored to daily banality, and were therefore delightful in themselves.

She was elated, and triumphant, and relieved. She had acted and created something. She had hazarded herself, and Brian had responded, and there it was. Brian's intent, open, good-natured look, as she rattled on about her beloved books: a look full of real interest. The look spoke of his own connection to the real world. It had happened. It was possible. It had happened.

They saw each other, after that, almost every day, or every other. Mostly they simply talked, and wandered between the hideouts Priya had found for her June and December daydreaming. The external walls of the Braddell apartment blocks were painted in clean government pastel—soft cream, faded orange, flat crayon green—and there were no unexpected spaces in their uniform grey interiors. But there were quiet corner spots where you could look out over the geometry of the Lego town, with its overspreading trees, its neat covered walkways criss-crossing between market, coffee shops, more apartment blocks, the sandy gold circles of playgrounds. Songbirds in corridors hung in cages from the ceiling, dangling nonchalantly over the edge of the parapet. And there were shifts of weather. Once they sat and listened to a thunderstorm reverberating in their ribcages. They made afternoon raids on the ixora bushes that lined the paths in the estate: twisting the red stems, pushing the stamens at their hearts, and pulling out tiny, thin piston-like threads capped with large, surprising globes of nectar.

It was a change for Brian, who said he was used to spending his holidays with Andrew, playing badminton and marbles, kicking a football about, retiring to their separate books.

"So long already and he's still sick. If I weren't hanging out with you, I'd be damn sian."

They were standing at the base of a stairwell in Priya's block, steps twisting skyward over their heads in a towering concrete ribbon. A week had passed since they'd first met, though with their hours together stretching out at leisure each day, it felt as though it had been longer.

"I used to want a brother," Priya said. "Or sister. I kept begging my parents for one."

"Aiyah, it's no big deal lah. I guess it's good there's someone to play games with." Brian had a sudden thought. "It's a bit weird to talk about him to you like this, you know. Because, my family and at school, everyone knows him, even the guys in the ping pong club know him 'cos he's in my year. And he's quite famous in school anyway lah. So it's a bit weird that you don't know him, but you know me." He met the fixed brown of her eyes, and felt a kind of pleasing, creeping consciousness of himself.

"What's he like? Is he like you?"

"Yah, I guess." Brian had never really thought about this much, except in relation to the stock subject of discussion at family gatherings: "But he's damn smart lah, much smarter than me. Always studying some more, he'll go and find all these extra things, not even storybooks or what, maths and science, not even homework also, and bring home to read for fun. Since Primary Four, for exams he always gets high marks, every paper more than 90. Mine are okay, but his are damn high. Next year when he goes secondary school, confirm it's a top one."

"Where do you want to go?"

"Don't know. Probably stay in St. Alex lorh." He assumed that he'd drift into the brother school of his primary school.

"All boys again? So boring! Hey, you should go to a mixed school, and then if I went to the same one, we'd be at the same school. We could see each other every day."

"That would be cool. That would be really great."

He was surprised by the solidity of this image, and by a flash of the distant glamour of being fifteen, and his face lit up with real enthusiasm. Enclosed in the safe grey tunnel of the stairwell, Priya looked at him, and the electric sympathy of friendship mixed with the thought, again, that he was really rather beautiful. There was a coiled-spring energy in the movement of his arm, from the line of his sleeve to his long brown fingers. She found herself taking his hand. His fingers curled round hers, and they smiled at each other in a flush of newness.

Theirs were clumsy embraces. Bits touched bits, absurdly. They were children, after all, covered all over in soft child skin, sticky with a Singaporean day of sweat, just on the threshold—if not yet tipped over—of unutterable self-consciousness. Brian was wearing his usual get-up of flip-flops and some cheap pasar malam T-shirt and those dirty green shorts that didn't do his toothpick boy legs any favours. As for Priya, bright-eyed, pudgy, round in the belly but not yet in the breast, it was some years before fashion would blip onto her radar. Grubby children, not magazine-perfect starlets. This afternoon they were all lips and hands and cloudless disbelief, comic and grandiose.

Brian had to be called to dinner twice. He clicked the television off and hurried over. Auntie Lay Choo, his father's younger sister, stood at the table, unfolding waxy brown paper packets. "This chicken rice is from a new stall near my work there," she announced. "You all must try and say whether good or not, maybe next time buy from there instead of Avenue 1."

Lay Choo was a small, energetic woman with dense waves of hair like her brother. But while Kim Seng wore his combed down and rigidly parted on the left, hers splayed out around her face like a stylised sunburst. She worked for a popular chain of shoe shops. Brian liked her. She dropped in now and then in the evening, and usually brought takeaway, which saved the boys some washing up; and her blunt talkativeness relieved the humid silence of the dinner table.

She measured up particularly well against Brian and Andrew's other aunts and uncles. Auntie Lay Peng, for instance, their father's oldest sister, was given to much stroking of Brian's arms and pinching of his thighs, and she invariably referred to him, cooingly, the vowels stretching in her mouth, as "Brai-Brai". (His brother was "Andy-boy".) This had all been bad enough when they were younger, but now that they were twelve it was unbearable.

And then there was Uncle Teck Sam, their mother's brother, who never paid any attention to the twins, except in certain leering, knowing comments, which triggered aggressive laughter from other uncles. Not that this really counted as speaking to the boys, because they never quite understood what was so funny, and they weren't meant to, either. Once Brian had a squeezy Doraemon figure on him, about five centimetres high, from one of those plastic bubbles that the machine by the bakery dispensed for twenty cents a piece. He had hoped for a top—one of the other guys had got a really cool one, wings unfurling in a sparkly black and orange blur as it spun—but Doraemon wasn't too bad either, except that its round blue earless head started Teck Sam going. "That thing!" he exclaimed. "Made by Japanese. You know where they come from or not, the Japanese?" Brian shook his head. "Long time ago, ten Chinese women were lost on the island, and ten monkeys came and raped them—and they gave birth to the first Japanese!" Brian recoiled, and his uncle laughed; he coloured angrily, and his uncle laughed some more. Later he learned—hating it—to feign knowingness, just to contain the laughter, but he could never quite join in.

It was a close thing between these two and Mabel's mother, Auntie Poh Lian, for the position of the most irritating figure in the family pantheon. Whenever Brian came within Poh Lian's line of sight, she would immediately offer her sister an authoritative appraisal of his appearance: "Aiyoh, Ling ah, Brian's hair grow until so long like that. Must tell him to cut, otherwise look like secret society gangster like that." He was so skinny, he needed to put on weight; he had become so tall already, next time he would be so much taller than his father; but his legs were not so long as this Keng Yong's son whose piano teacher's daughter's netball teammate was in Jasmine's class. Even ostensibly positive remarks grated—Brian would much rather not hear assessments of himself at all.

Against this competition, if Auntie Lay Choo had a tendency to chatter on a little too much, and to direct somewhat banal questions to the twins without really listening to the answers—well, these were trivial enough faults in the general scheme. At twenty-seven, she sometimes seemed cut from a different generation of cloth from Brian's parents. Her speech was peppered with references to a kaleidoscope of friends, places, events and activities, which the boys and their parents had trouble tracking. They formed a foreign world which never really intersected with Teo family occasions, although Nurul, a frequently mentioned colleague, had once put in an appearance at Chinese New Year. Brian had been rather confused about how to address her. "Auntie" was the obvious choice, given her age and her friendship with Lay Choo. But she had called herself plain Nurul, and his parents had, unusually, made none of those chivvying introductions in which the boys were ordered—mildly, but unmistakably—to acknowledge the superior status of adult visitors. ("Brian,

Andrew, call Auntie Joy!" and "Auntie Joy," they were to reply, with a suitably deferent nod.)

Now, at dinner, the others were slotted in tightly around Lay Choo. Stools shifted restlessly to accommodate Brian. It was a pinch even for four in the kitchen, but habit reserved the living room's dining table for smarter occasions, like birthdays or New Year. Brian felt hemmed in, with Mabel at his left elbow and Andrew jogging his right. He began to eat rather impatiently.

"Wah, just now the show very exciting is it? So engrossed."

Brian murmured vague assent. In fact, the onscreen intrigue had hardly registered. But Lay Choo had already moved to something else: "Looks like you are better now already, Andrew? Your mother and father were very worried, you know! Dengue fever is no joke, okay."

"Yah, better now, Auntie."

"No more fever already," Mabel added.

"Doctor said should be better after a week lah," Brian's mother said. "Actually when she said don't need to go hospital I was less worried already, don't have to stay in hospital means not so serious one." She spoke laconically, far from the early horror when she'd thought she might lose her child. "Mabel has been very good with helping, horh, Andrew? Thank you ah, Mabel. But I think now don't need already lah, make you come all the way to Braddell so leceh."

"Actually, Auntie," Mabel began, and stopped short.

She glanced urgently past Brian, at Andrew, who said nothing. "I don't mind, Auntie."

"No lah, now is your holidays some more."

"No really, Auntie, it's okay." She looked again at Andrew, who continued to eat silently.

"Andrew, luckily your dengue is during June holidays!" his father said. "Don't need MC. This year exams very important, PSLE, better don't miss school."

"Oh yah, PSLE horh. So next year secondary school already, right? So boys, where are you going?"

"Andrew should apply to Ashford Hall," Kim Seng said, pronouncing the name carefully. He was expressing high hopes here: children in Singapore were fed into a multi-tiered boilerhouse of academic assessment, which separated them into different grades, again and again, with ever subtler distinctions and refinements, until—according to official theory—each was deposited in an output tray reflecting their innate ability. The Primary School Leaving Examination or PSLE was a crucial component of this island-wide distillation process. It didn't just determine whether a child made it into the Express stream of secondary education (to be Normal was to fall off the edge of the known universe), but also which of the relentlessly ranked and re-ranked secondary schools they would enter. For obsessive, hawk-eyed parents, this said everything about where your (and your colleague's and your sister's and your neighbour's) twelve-year-old avatar stood in life, and how smooth their path would be toward those much coveted places, first in junior college, and then, one prayed, university.

A few stately giants among secondary schools spread their canopies far above the rest of the jostling undergrowth; and for boys, the undisputed lord of the jungle was the prestigious Ashford Hall, widely understood as a passport to the highest lifelong success.

"Wah, Ashford? Really ah? Ashford very high-pressure one, you know? My big boss, his nephew started Sec One this year, went to Nanyang Boys—wah, he says it's very stressful. But you boys are hardworking one, lah, can cope."

"Andrew will have no problem, I am sure," Brian's father told his sister with satisfaction. "Brian also, can try right? But Brian said before he wants to go with his friends to St. Alexander's."

The conversation was uncomfortably close to Brian's recent exchange with Priya in the stairwell. Some instinct kept her secret. He shrugged. "See how lah."

It was a humid night. In the twins' room, the table fan swung a blind, ponderous face from side to side, its blades cutting a narrow channel of relief through the heavy air. Mabel let herself in after helping with the dishes—a duty she had spared both boys for some weeks now. She turned the chair at the desk around, sat, and stared first at Andrew, who fiddled with his Rubik's Cube, and then at Brian, who said nothing.

Finally she turned back to Andrew. "Tomorrow morning I have a church outing. So I can't come until afternoon."

"Okay." One panel was almost green.

"You and Brian should come to church on Sunday. You'll learn a lot. Important things that even your parents or your teachers never tell you."

Brian groaned loudly. It seemed to him that some version of the God conversation took place, with dead regularity, whenever the cousins were alone. As if Mabel had a divine sales quota to fill. It was always the same: the demands for obedience thinly masked as concern. Tonight, in the frazzling heat, talk made Brian prickle with irritation. He wanted to be alone; or at any rate to sit in the hum of the fan and the click of Andrew's Cube, the closest to aloneness he could manage.

Andrew, for his part, was fundamentally uninterested in church: it was ritual and clutter. Mabel's efforts embarrassed him. But he heard a note of appeal in her voice, and was hesitant to join in Brian's open derision. "See how lah."

"No," Brian said. "I don't want to go. It's boring."

"You've never been," Mabel said crossly. "How do you know? You should try new things. Have you ever even stopped to ask yourself, am I missing out by not trying to find out about God? You shouldn't be closed-minded, it's not good for you."

"I've heard about this stuff before lah, at school also got, you know? St. Alex. Catholic school."

"But church is different lah. And Catholics are not exactly the same as Christians." She paused, uncertain that elaborating the finer points of theology would be persuasive.

"Aiyah, it's all the same thing. Jesus and Mary and all that. It's like going to school, have to wake up early in the morning and sit there and listen to some old man talking on and on, what for?" He looked to his brother to back him up, but Andrew was gazing diplomatically into a corner of the room. The possibility of his defection was alarming. "Andrew, you're still sick, right? Like that how to go?"

"Aiyah, it's not taxing at all! He can go. Anyway, he's better now."

"Is it? Then you can stop coming every day, right? Nobody wants you here nagging about your god."

Mabel coloured. "Andrew still needs help," she muttered to her hands. The line sank in the dense, wet air.

The table fan reached the end of a pendulous sweep and cranked noisily into reverse. They sat for a moment, and then the doorbell rang, prompting a jangle of keys, and the clang and rattle of the padlock and the grill on the front door. Lay Choo bustled in. "Mabel, your mother's here."

Mabel left in a cloud of wounded anger.

"She's trying to be nice, you know," Andrew said. "She thinks she's being nice."

"Aiyah, told her so many times already, we're not interested. Don't know why she thinks if she just keeps bringing it up, over and over and over, we'll suddenly want to go."

"Yah…" Andrew tried to think of the right angle. "You know, I think she doesn't really have friends to hang out with." He meant this by way of mitigation.

"No wonder, right. Everything always god, god, god, church, church, church. I don't get it. It's weird."

Andrew sensed that the point was lost. He shrugged. "Of course lah, it's Mabel what."

They shared small, complicit grins. Brian was reassured. He sat back in the lull of the fan, finally left to his thoughts about the book. He had finished it now, and was both chilled and thrilled by the image of a heart first swapped out for illicit powers, and then hidden, like treasure, from pursuit by dangerous others. He thought also of Priya, and wondered what she was doing. He did not think to say anything to Andrew. He thought in pictures and not in any practical detail.

Much later on, Priya remembered and forgot Brian, in quite a different way from how he remembered and forgot her. Events as such escaped him, but their hours together became suffused, for him, with tints of romance, wistfulness, tragedy, that became the full substance of his association with Priya Menon. She was what he had lost. She, on the other hand, understood the entire business as a textureless sequence of things that had happened, concluding in a lesson to be learned. Any memory of how she had *felt* that June only increased her contempt for her own childish self. Brian himself sank beneath consideration. He was a delusion, fractured by fate, which it would be worse than useless to re-piece.

So she was thrown when, in the March of 1998, the news reports were published, and his face was everywhere, almost familiar, but impossible to identify.

It was, in fact, the second time pictures of him had made the rounds. He had also been in all the papers four years earlier. But Priya had no interest in the government's annual awards to its "scholars", those overachieving schoolkids, chosen for cultivation as young mandarins, who received full funding for their Ivy League and Oxbridge undergraduate courses, and became contractually bound to—were greasily accelerated up—the civil service ladder. Every year, among the few hundred selected for this privilege, a tinier handful still were anointed elite among the elite. These were photographed in suits and smiles, a trio or a quartet of smart, toothy marionettes, and splashed across *The Straits Times*. Nothing had registered with Priya then; she had simply turned the page.

Now, though, the story was irresistible—SUICIDE SCHOLAR 'HID UNSTABLE TENDENCIES'—and why, she asked herself, was a curious bubble of recognition welling in her as she looked at this dead bright young man? His name meant nothing, she had never met him, but at the same time she felt bodily certain that she had. There were no clues in the text: the stratospheric schools he'd attended, the awards he'd won, his unfinished Master's degree in Mathematics. Assurances from the Civil Service Board that scholarship holders were not only the very best academic talents, but also underwent stringent psychological assessment; every care was taken with taxpayer money, but mistakes did happen; the system took into account the possibility of a small percentage of error; some people were tragically unable to cope with stress in their personal lives. The bereaved family had no comment.

She stared again at his face, and forgot about it for most of the rest of the day. That evening, walking home from the bus stop, she thought how much more pleasant it was now, when the hot grey fuzz of the year before had lifted from the air, even if the Sumatran forests were still, by all accounts, burning, and the connection appeared in her mind all at once. The suicide guy. It was that random and embarrassing boy, Brian had been his name, he had—she surprised herself by retrieving the useless fact from some unlit mental recess—he had a brother who looked just like him. It was the brother, whom she had, indeed, never met.

This feeling of recognition was the only evidence that she had ever met Brian himself. Nothing else in her life corroborated it. No one knew about him: he had been a story beneath telling. It was odd to think on his reality, somewhere out there, maybe living nearby still (even odder), and on the reality of his grief (surely he was grieving). His parents, silent players in her childhood drama, known only as objects of resentment, now given this extra dimension: they must be grieving too. She thought of the unknown brother, a stranger figure, whose sensitivities were being publicly canvassed, and wondered how he had been, that brother in that family. She felt pity, and then a flush of muted anger, ebbing even as it surged. An anger at her pity, an anger which intensified her pity. She did not want to feel sorry for them, she had no right to and they had no right to it, and yet she did feel sorry for them. She did.

The twins were locking the front gate as Mabel arrived. Traffic had been slow, and she was out of breath from the bus-stop-to-doorstop canter. From down the corridor the brothers were hard to distinguish, the same thin frames, each in identical shorts and a T-shirt, one holding a tube of shuttlecocks, the other with Yonex rackets slung over his shoulder.

"Hullo," Andrew said.

"We're playing badminton," said Brian.

The question showed in Mabel's face—a little later, and she'd have been shut out of an empty flat.

"We didn't know you were coming today."

"'Cos normally you'd be here by now, and you hadn't come," Andrew added quickly. "Why don't you come and watch?"

"Sure you should be playing or not? So soon after dengue? What if you get worse again?"

"Yah, yah, he's okay already lah."

"Should be fine."

"Okay, I'd better come in case anything happens to you."

Not knowing the way, Mabel trailed after the boys, through the estate, to the main road. They stopped at a pedestrian crossing. The sun blanketed them; it was another unpleasantly hot day, but even so, Andrew was glad to be out of the flat at last and standing under the sky. His legs and arms felt unused and ready. It had been easy for Brian to sell him on a game.

Mabel fixed her gaze on the lit figure of the red man at the crossing, mentally tracing and re-tracing its tiny outline. Emptying her mind. When the lights shifted it took her a few moments to respond.

The hall in the Community Centre was high-ceilinged and airy and shuttered. The boys rapidly shed bits of gear, their unzipped racket covers sliding to the floor, and assumed their stations at opposite ends of a court, two magnetic poles straining apart with competitive energy.

Andrew was the more technically competent player, but not by much, and after the dengue Brian was in better shape. Brian felt good: he'd forgotten how much he liked these games. At first his grip on his racket was too tight, and he had trouble matching his feel for the dimensions of the court to his sense of his own pace and strength. His shots went out, wide, into the net—he lost five early, easy points. But he was enjoying the pure pleasure of motion, and he grew steadily more relaxed and controlled. Suddenly he placed a series of assured safe shots. He began propelling himself to difficult returns with cunning bursts of energy, prolonging the rally at unexpected points. Andrew, run tired, a little confused, mishit an easy shot out of the court.

Success. Brian seized the service and pressed forward, cautiously, but keeping up the momentum. They were rapidly level. Brian became excited: his approach worked. If he could just take a good lead now. He paused to wipe his face with his T-shirt—was surprised to find it soaked—and moved to serve again, the same motion, again, but this time he had been thinking too much about the score, and his wrist action was mistimed. The shuttlecock went into the net.

With this piece of luck, Andrew caught a second wind. He knocked the shuttlecock into an awkward high spot in Brian's backhand, pulling a point ahead that way, then two, three, in quick succession. Even after Brian managed to break the pattern, he remained on the back foot; by the time he struggled back into service, the game felt as good as over. He crawled up a half-hearted two points before control returned to Andrew, who made fifteen with ease.

"Play again?"

"Yah."

Mabel had found herself a bench by the courts and was trying to read. Today she had with her a tract on prayer, written in breezy American, which had been loaned to her by a friendly woman at church. But the lighting in the hall was poor, and the metallic ring of shuttlecocks in sweet spots, the sharply muffled squeak of trainers on wood floor, kept cutting across her attention. The bench was of an inconvenient width, too—if she sat with her back up against the wall, her knees came short of the end, so that her shins stuck out; if she sat forward, with her feet on the ground, most of her weight came uncomfortably down on one wooden slat. She shifted and shifted, keeping the book open, though the text dissolved and re-formed into a blurred, irregular geometry. Now and then she tuned in to the twins' game, but she had no interest in sport; she didn't understand what she was meant to look for.

She closed her eyes against the noise. Dear Lord God. Please. The thought had no end. She decided to buy herself a packet drink. There must be a vending machine somewhere. She wandered out of the hall and into the entrance lobby. There it was, boxy, humming. She dropped two coins in and pressed the button under the display for Yeo's chrysanthemum tea. The machine gave an electric purr and the yellow packet fell heavily. She retrieved it, returned to her unstable perch on the bench, stabbed the little foil circle with the straw, drank. The tea was sticky sweet.

She managed to drag the performance of drinking out for a good ten minutes, but at the end of it the boys were still pivoting and circling on the court, about their common axis of eagerness, and it was necessary to find something else to do. Reluctantly, at last, she considered the problem of Andrew. There was a good half of the June break left, which she did not want to spend at home. Home was difficult. Her little sister Jasmine was far too young to be of any use, her mother had been even angrier than usual lately, and—most importantly, of course—she ought to seek activity. A purpose-driven life was part of God's design for those on earth. It was rather unglamorous to tag along behind a younger cousin—the girls at school would surely sneer if they knew, the trendy clique with their streaked hair and their junior college boyfriends. But, Mabel told herself, the Lord worked in mysterious ways; she must have been directed to Andrew's care for a reason. And he was fairly grown-up for twelve, wasn't he, and seemed to like her—not that it mattered, her task was her task.

The problem of Andrew was really, of course, the problem of Brian. Quite apart from his tiresome hostility, her accidental knowledge about him disturbed and disgusted her. But she didn't want to dwell on it unduly: such thoughts corrupted, and the Lord must have His own plan for punishing sin. At any rate she could also see how it might be useful. Brian would be away now and then, and there was her opportunity. Today was not the pattern of things; he could not want to play badminton all the time.

And maybe Andrew wouldn't either. He might not be a believer as yet, but with him the door to fellowship was at least ajar; he seemed to have an inkling of the possibility of God's love, a faint appreciation of the merits of her Christian life. Perhaps he would ask her for a book on Christ. This idea was not so dangerous, was it, when he had liked her selections from the library so far. He might have questions, and then—this must be what God intended—it would fall to her to take him through the parables, patiently and carefully, like Pastor Hong did with the Sunday school class. Andrew was smart. He would recognise wisdom when he saw it. She had a vision of Brian approaching one morning, rackets in hand, and his brother waving him away in favour of hearing more about the Lord. Preferring to share in the secrets of righteous knowledge with her, Mabel.

Some minutes passed before she looked up, suddenly aware of silence. The court was empty. She got to her feet, turning this way and that, but there was no sign of the boys in the dim hall. Their gear had vanished. They wouldn't be in the showers—they hadn't brought towels with them, or any change of clothes. Could they have gone to the toilets? Perhaps they were in the lobby, for packet drinks of their own?

She padded quickly over. The only person there was a thin old man, sweeping the floor and grumbling to himself in Bahasa Melayu. Outside, the sky was white.

They set off for home in high spirits, each with a game under his belt to glory in. Less than two minutes from the last shot and already they were reminiscing about moments of prowess or luck, and vowing greater future victories. Brian wondered when he could schedule another match. It would have to wait for another opportunity like today's, when Priya had been spirited away by a family event. It was a good problem to have: too many pleasant things to arrange around one another. They made it to the foot of their block before Andrew remembered Mabel.

"Oh, shit," they said as they turned back, but laughingly, still charged with adrenaline. Both were still trilling with amusement as they reappeared in the Community Centre.

Brian spotted Mabel first: she had just replaced the handset on the small, orange-topped plastic payphone, and was reinserting the coin it duly spat out. They moved toward her, and he realised as he watched that she was frantically punching the number for their flat.

"Hullo, Mabel," he said, gaily, in her ear. She started, and dropped the phone. The boys burst into laughter.

Her face was flushed red, her mouth set with effort. "You left without me." She wanted to sound stern, accusatory.

She wanted to look calm.

"Sorry," Andrew said, grinning.

"We forgot you were there."

"We were so excited by the game."

"And then we almost got home and then we were like, shit, where is Mabel?"

"So we came back."

"Were you calling us? Special delivery, we came super quickly."

The twins laughed again. Mabel bit her lip. "It's not funny, okay."

"Sorry," Andrew repeated. "But we're here now, yah?"

"And come on lah, Mabel, it's not that far, we only went a short while ago, at most twenty minutes only."

"Whatever it is, it's very inconsiderate."

"Aiyah," Brian said. "You should have known we finished already what! Next time pay attention lah." He paused. "It's allowed, right? Bible doesn't say cannot watch badminton?"

At this, despite himself, Andrew let out a thin giggle. Mabel's heart contracted with a cold stab. "Shut up, Brian."

"Aiyah, relax a bit lah!" Brian said, enjoying himself. He picked up the book Mabel had placed by the phone. "*How to Talk to God: A Guide for Teens*." He began to flip through it. "See, I'm sure it doesn't say anything about—"

Mabel grabbed at the book. They tussled briefly; and there was a loud ripping sound, as the pages in Brian's fingers came apart. "Oh. Oh, shit." He let go. Jagged-edged flaps of paper fell to the floor.

Mabel gave a short, furious cry, and began picking up the pieces. The boys joined her in subdued silence. She accepted the scraps they handed her without meeting their gaze, her thin frame held away at a defensive angle. Her eyes were wet, reddened.

"Sorry, Mabel."

"Yeah, sorry."

She stood up and methodically folded the last of the torn pages into the back of the book. When she finally spoke it was in a tight and withering voice. "Take me back. Now."

They complied. Mabel deliberately stayed a few paces behind the boys, refusing to look at or speak to them. Neither really tried to engage her, or to speak to each other.

Despite the signs promising heavy fines, someone had urinated in the lift. As they rode up in the cramped space, the dank smell seemed worse than ever. Brian did his best not to gag. He felt some small relief as they reached their front door, and Andrew undid the various locks. He was mildly ashamed of his part with the book, but it didn't look like Mabel was going to shout at them or make a scene, and perhaps after sulking for an evening she would forget about it. He moved to follow Andrew into the flat, and was startled when his cousin gripped his elbow to keep him back.

"I've seen you," she said quietly.

"What?"

"I've seen you," she repeated. "With that dirty—*fat*—*apunehneh*. I can't believe you would—it's disgusting, you're really disgusting." She met his plain surprise with a look of hard satisfaction, and stepped past him into the flat. When he had recovered himself enough to go in, Mabel and Andrew were peaceably arranged on the sofas, watching television. Mabel ignored Brian for the rest of the day—which made little difference, as he, in any case, could not think what he should say.

That was the last of Mabel's visits. Over dinner she cheerfully informed everyone that, in her opinion, Andrew was so much better now, and no longer needed her help, so if Auntie and Uncle didn't mind, she wouldn't come round any more.

Brian later assumed that Mabel had drawn his parents aside, unnoticed. In fact, she said nothing to them. A dry mention to her mother was enough to do the trick. Auntie Poh Lian, all aflutter, called her sister the next day: prompted only, of course, by her deep concern for the family's well-being. She didn't enjoy talking of such shameful things, but she knew Poh Ling would realise how serious it was, and how bad it must look. If it were her own daughter who had behaved in this way, she would feel so ashamed; and the worst thing was, if Mabel had seen Brian doing hanky-panky with this fat Indian in public, who knew how many neighbours must have seen it too? Everyone knew boy-girl relationships were a danger in secondary school, but you didn't expect it to start so early—and in Brian's PSLE year some more, Poh Ling must be especially worried. She mustn't think it meant they were bad parents who didn't know how to control their kids properly, oh no, it was probably the fashion to give your children a lot of freedom these days; although Poh Lian herself had always thought it was important not to just blindly follow fashion. When it came to her own girls, even though she taught them good Christian principles, she thought it was better to restrict them a little bit—better not to take chances, because once children began to rebel, it was very hard to get them to come back to you.

Poh Ling said very little. She was disoriented by the idea of her son "doing hanky-panky" with anyone—an essentially inconceivable idea, given unwelcome solidity by the fatness and Indianness of this mystery girl. These were distracting, almost mesmerising, facts. She wondered how best to communicate them to her husband. She considered herself a practical parent, and a flexible one, too. This business with Brian must stop, of course, but preferably without drama—something she worried Kim Seng had an occasional tendency to indulge.

She was roused by a high edge in Poh Lian's voice. "…you know, some of these Malay and Indian girls are very advanced one, thirteen, fourteen, already having babies. And you better be careful, when he is older, make sure he meets some good Chinese girls, otherwise next time you get an Indian daughter-in-law, then you know. I asked Mabel if this one was one of the fair-skinned type, you know some of them are not so dark, but Mabel said no, she was one of the very black-black ones." She bubbled over into nervous laughter. Poh Ling felt a surge of irritation.

"Okay," she said. "Thanks, Lian, thanks for telling me about this. We must talk to Brian. Everything okay with you?"

"Oh, yes, yes, it's all fine, good to have Mabel back home also, I always get worried when she goes out so much. You just never know what kind of influence there will be on them, horh? But good that she told me this lah, shows she has good values. I just wanted to make sure you knew what your son has been up to—"

"Yes, thanks, thanks," Poh Ling repeated. "Okay. Don't forget we have booked two tables at Jin Loong for Ma's birthday."

"Yes, of course. Don't worry ah, Ling, I'm sure it will be okay with Brian, he is still young, just talk to him firmly."

"We will. Okay, bye."

From the moment Mabel hissed at him on the doorstep, a small ball of worry had lodged itself in Brian. It tangled and grew as he tossed it about in what he knew of his parents. Anxious threads snarled themselves in his chest and in his throat. He was dismayed, but not surprised, when, two evenings later, his mother asked him to come to her bedroom.

It was not a space in which Brian was generally welcome. He stepped nervously in—his mother closing the door against an incurious Andrew—and stood in the thick grave silence of his father's scrutiny. Kim Seng's eyes, behind the large lenses of his blocky plastic glasses, had a perpetual slight goggle, and his mouth tended to hang just a little open in the square of his face. (It was fair to say the twins owed their more decisive looks mostly to their mother.) Someone else might have found this gaze comical, but Brian did not. He returned it momentarily, and then looked away, already anticipating shame.

"Brian. Your cousin Mabel says she saw you with this—Indian girl."

Brian could not have told you how he knew that his parents would disapprove of Priya. It wasn't that he didn't notice the clues—he absorbed them, bathed in them even. But isolating them was beyond his powers. He did not know, could not imagine, parents who did not stud every other conversation with talk of the ultimate danger—of children "distracted" from their homework and exams. In the context of their sons, girls were spoken of only in voices cloudy with shame: and shame, therefore, was the nature of girls. He saw nothing unusual in the persistence with which they itemised other people by ethnicity ("The salesgirl was a Malay", "She spoke to the ang moh", "There were five Chinese and two mangali") or in their self-satisfied jibes, accompanying every drive through Little India, about the danger of knocking its dark-skinned inhabitants over at night. He had learned, in school, that a beneficent "racial and religious harmony" prevailed in Singapore; and since it did, this must be the face of it. This was simply how his parents talked, this was just what they laughed at. It was obvious to him, foundational. That it was also utterly incompatible with the fact of Priya, was something he grasped instantly, with all the certainty, all the analysis, and all the capacity for criticism or resistance, of a plant turning toward sunlight.

Because he knew this, once his father spoke, the session that stretched before Brian seemed immediately, enormously redundant. He stiffened in dread of a dirty-fingered rummage through the details. He could learn nothing in the process; he could only be confirmed in his own humiliation.

"Who is this Indian? Where does she come from?"

"My friend Priya," Brian began. And then stopped in confusion. He didn't have answers to these questions, at least not the kind of answers his father sought.

"What sort of friend is this? Cannot be at school, yours is a boys' school. Where are you finding this type of friend?"

Where indeed? he wondered, with miserable clarity. The impossibility of it was obvious now. The fantasy aisle of a second-hand bookstore, the inside of a playground's make-believe animal, a closed grey stairwell to the stars: how could he have thought the world might contain enough secret passages in which to hide them? "We met in—" he tried, but he couldn't go on, he couldn't expose that afternoon and its laughter to the acid air of his father's contempt.

His silence annoyed his father. "Brian, your father is trying to be patient with you, but this is very serious. Who started this monkey business? Must be this girl's family never teach her properly. Don't let people say your father and mother never teach you properly. Mabel saw you doing all kinds of things in public. In front for everyone to see. With a fat Indian!"

Despite himself, Brian let out a sob.

"Brian," Poh Ling said, in what she meant to be a soothing voice. "We just don't want you to be led astray—"

"—yah, these Indians are very good at talking, full of hot air—"

"—when this girl tries to encourage you to misbehave, you must step back and think about your parents. We only want what is best for you. You are still too young for this kind of thing."

"That's why!" his father exclaimed. "So young already and doing this kind of thing. You better not go and make some girl pregnant."

White hot shock showed in Brian's face. His mother tried to steer the conversation to safer ground. "Now is your PSLE year, very important for your future, your whole life.

Your father and mother work so hard so you can have a good life, don't need to worry about rice bowl every day. Don't say we are not reasonable. We don't like scolding you also. All we ask is you concentrate on your studies for now. Next time after you pass all your exams, go university and have a good job, then you can think about having a girlfriend." She paused. "Your father and mother will not always be around, Brian, don't make us disappointed."

Brian stared at the floor. The last line was irrefutable. He wasn't persuaded by any of this, so much as winded under the crushing knowledge of his own smallness and ingratitude. He hated this knowledge, which clung viciously to all open disagreement with his mother and his father. He had no arguments in his favour other than his feelings about Priya—the warm and prickling aliveness, the joyful unfolding—fragile phantoms, all—and he knew it would be stupid to speak of them. They were nothing against the weight of his parents' responsibility for his entire existence. Disobedience was unthinkable. He took a deep breath.

"Sorry," he said.

His parents exchanged glances. "Good," his father said, after a moment's silence. "Good that you realised you made a mistake. But cannot just say sorry, sorry is just saying only, you must make sure you don't do it again."

"Yes, Pa."

"Don't talk to this what, Bina or what, any more. Better

that you don't mix with this kind of people, don't know how their father and mother brought them up also, young girl already behaving like this."

"Yes, Pa."

"Do you promise your father and mother?"

"Yes, Mum; yes, Pa."

"Okay. Good." Kim Seng gestured abruptly for his son to leave.

"Good boy," Poh Ling said. "You know it is only because your father and mother want what is best for you, that we must sometimes be firm with you." She opened the door to the room, smiling at him, pleased that matters had been handled with a minimum of fuss. "Dinner in a few minutes, I just reheat yesterday's chicken. Andrew," she called. "Andrew! Dinner soon."

Kim Seng could remember his own childhood in the crowded kampung village. Days among the muddy dirt tracks and the peeling wood walls. Mangy dogs and pungent bullock carts and everywhere mosquitoes. A meal was frequently the flesh from a single chicken thigh, parcelled out among all the brothers and sisters. Nights brought terror, the brewery smell of his father's coming-home breath. His own sons had been well-fed and comfortable all their lives. He had never raised a hand in anger. No one could say he wasn't good to them.

Brian lay in bed that night listening to Andrew's breathing, waiting for his brother to fall asleep so that he could have some privacy in which to cry. But he drifted off, himself, before the moment arrived. He slept well, and woke the next morning to his brother drawing blinds, the sun a yolky orange disc, low and rising in the sky.

Elsewhere that June there were bare cells, impossible questions in icy rooms, honest answers met with blows. Vincent Cheng and the other conspirators perjured themselves, against themselves. The nation accepted their confessions and averted its eyes from the confessors (and the cells, and the questions, and the blows). It was safest to act as though nothing had happened or changed.

Brian avoided the Frankie Wong bookstore for a while. It didn't offer much in the way of the non-fiction Andrew preferred, anyway, so the boys made trips to the local library instead. The day when Brian had arranged to next meet Priya quietly came, and just as quietly went. The boys kicked a chatek about in the void deck. It was hypnotic and comforting: the slap of the weight on the side of his foot; up and down, the rhythmic flash of fuchsia feathers. He was better at it than was Andrew. They played a lot of badminton.

    He was in the lobby of the Community Centre after one of their games—Andrew had just dashed off to the toilet—

when he heard a voice call his name. He took a moment to place it, and then Priya was standing in front of him, beaming. "Brian!" she repeated. "I wondered what happened to you! Did you have to go somewhere—were you sick?" She moved a hand towards him in greeting. His shoulders froze and he twisted away.

"What's wrong?"

Her eyes brimmed with bright concern. They were pretty, he thought with alarm; she was pretty. He put a palm over his face and looked at her through his fingers.

"Brian?"

"Sorry," he said, uncovering his face. "Sorry." There was an uncomprehending silence, and then he said, all in a rush, "Sorry, I can't meet you any more, my parents don't allow me, sorry, Priya."

"Don't allow you? What did you tell them? How do they know—" The question was too embarrassing to complete. They stood mirroring each other. "But—but we can be friends, right?"

"I can't, my parents don't allow me," he said again. "Sorry."

"How can they don't allow us to be friends?"

"I don't know, they just don't, they don't like you."

"How can they don't like me?"

"They don't, they made me promise, I can't, Priya."

"But why not? Why don't they like me? What's wrong with me?"

"You're Indian," he said, miserable.

She stared at him. Her face worked in all different directions at once. For an awful moment Brian thought she was going to cry; and then her look fixed into pure scorn. He returned it with hangdog helplessness, and she turned and walked rapidly away.

"Sorry," he repeated, his heart firing in sharp staccato code, but she had gone.

"What?" Andrew was at his elbow.

"Nothing."

"I heard you say sorry, who were you saying sorry to?"

"No one," Brian said quickly. "It was no one." He picked his tube of shuttlecocks off the floor. "Let's go home."

# MARCH 1998

THE PICTURE WAS a scan: of a Polaroid, it looked like, from its squarish proportions and its thick white borders. Much of the space in it was occupied by the head and shoulders of a young Caucasian man. He had a thin, freckled face, set with wide but sleepy blue-grey eyes, and framed by dark hair that curled wildly around his ears. He looked straight into the camera, and the curve of his lips was half cheeky, half shy. A small gap showed between his front teeth. His shoulders were bare.

Andrew was also in the picture. His face was partly obscured, and tilted gently downward, but it was clearly him, pressed up close behind the unknown man, kissing the slope of his neck. Brian recognised the hands, so like his own, brushing pale collarbone and chest. The expression on Andrew's face was less familiar: a slow almost-smile, peaceful half-lidded eyes. He looked like the exhalation of a long-drawn breath.

To Brian's knowledge, his parents looked at the photograph only once. He'd shown it to them together with the email from Hwee Leng. They did not ask to see it, nor did they refer to it, again.

Brian himself, however, spent a lot of time studying it. It was frustratingly small on the computer monitor, a box within a box. Items in the background offered themselves with deceptive clarity: pinned up on a corkboard there were other photographs, and the dismembered edges of brightly coloured bits of paper, yellow, orange and aquamarine, printed with snatches of black text. But when Brian zoomed in, the tiny sharp figures expanded into blurs of pixellation, the illusion of resolution destroyed.

Most likely these fragments were of flyers and posters for college events, glossy and anonymous, revealing no more than the bland personal effects which returned with Andrew's body. (Notebooks of matrices, equations, graphs; jeans, T-shirts and woolly pullovers; a small collection of pop music; a Discman. A computer with its hard drive wiped.) Brian wasn't looking for answers. He just found the picture—not exactly comforting, but something close to it. Despite everything. Whatever else it also was, it was a totem of his own ignorance and of Andrew's reality. These both seemed important. He mistrusted his own unaided remembrance.

Inevitably he sought other pictures of his brother. Bleached and grainy scenes from the zoo: the twins about eight, all twiggy limbs and mussed and sweaty hair, fidgeting under the stare of the lens. They had shared all their clothes back then, and though one boy distinguished himself through a missing front tooth, Brian wasn't always sure whom he was looking at. (In some photographs, this difficulty was resolved by the presence of Jojo, a pale blue stuffed dog with a solemn face and a red bow tie, over whom Brian had exercised a tyrannical possessiveness.) He found crowded shots from forgotten family dinners with his father's five siblings and their sundry children—the twins always looking out together, an island of repetitive simplicity in the choppy sea of faces. A single holiday album recorded a long weekend spent in Malacca when they were thirteen.

The family photographs began, here, to dwindle. Andrew appeared instead at a string of competitions: holding trophies and plaques aloft, in his sports kit or smart school blazer and tie. On class trips—in the thickness of mangroves, in front of Parliament House—he grinned out of circles of friends. Some of these boys Brian recognised, some he didn't. More familiar to him was the short sequence of scenes, from when they were eighteen, of both brothers hanging out together, eating prata, or sitting on the beach at East Coast Park. Hwee Leng appeared in these pictures too, her face flushed and happy; and in a few, Brian saw that mouthy guy who used to tag along with Andrew—Ming Wei, that was his name.

And then, of course, the newspaper cuttings their parents had preserved—telling the tale of the boy from the Housing Development Board heartlands, whose impending journey, first to England's finest university and then to a gilded position in the state bureaucracy, served as proof, if proof were needed, of the fairness of Singapore's meritocracy. Andrew's hair was still cropped close to his skull in those press shots: he had only lately finished three months of Basic Military Training, though as a government "scholar" he was permitted to postpone the remaining two years of his National Service obligation until after he had acquired his degrees.

As if in response to this brush with baldness, Andrew wore a thick mop in the university pictures. These he had explained to Brian and their parents in light and rapid tones. They were taken in places with curiously diminutive names, like the homes of woodland animals in some pastoral children's book: on the grassy Backs along the river Cam; by the Van of Life, which sold midnight burgers to hungry students; in Maypoles and Mitres and other dim and foreign pubs. Andrew was surrounded by other students in fleeces and in stark striped scarfs, laughing toothily, smoking, holding forth; and by forests of pint glasses, emptied to white traces of foam or filled with brassy brown beer. (Brian looked for that other young man, with his dark curly hair, and could not find him.) Time was partitioned in novel ways in this world: red and yellow leaves were assigned to Michaelmas, a snow-covered bicycle to Lent.

Brian had found his brother's explanations difficult and dazzling. After a week in the barracks, with its ceaseless, pounding labour, the vampiric drain of its night shifts, the constant fear of some officer's caprice, he was always bone-tired, hungry, holding himself back. Against this, the carnival of a life that Andrew brought home in his assured summer anecdotes was never quite conceivable. Brian leaned back into the sofa, exhaustedly rubbing his own botak head—for *he* still had to keep his hair short—and let the patter run over him in rills.

But in a sense the change was not so great. Since their paths had split in secondary school, his brother's world had filled with bright and unusual things, and Andrew himself had altered. He stood differently, walked with a different gait, spoke with a new quickness and a refinement of accent that all but eliminated confusion between them. For a long time, Andrew had been strange to Brian. The sudden Britishisms and the casual talk of European cities were merely extensions of this established fact—the very continuity of his strangeness was paradoxically familiar. And whatever these shiny add-ons, the context of them was clear. The context was Andrew, whom he had always known.

Few of Andrew's friends came to his wake. Many of them, like Andrew, were government "scholars" or Ashford alumni or both, reading prestigious degrees in famous universities in Europe, the United States, Japan. Three of them called. Others dropped Brian safe, generic messages (his email address had clearly been somehow shuffled among them), explaining that they could not afford the airfare for such a brief return, and offering stiff condolences.

Brian didn't know how to read their reticence. Even Hwee Leng, whose sympathies on the matter (or any matter) were in no doubt, spoke haltingly, without her usual fluency, when the phone call finally came. Perhaps he could expect no more from the others. Perhaps, young and privileged to the last, death was simply not in their vocabulary.

Still it bothered him. Was anyone keeping away? There must be more than this handful of old classmates in the country. And those who were there made him anxious; he thought he could feel them exchanging looks and words, stained with knowledge—a prickly, vibratory feeling, like the blind sonar detection of a bat. He didn't always commit himself to what Hwee Leng said, less because he doubted her, exactly, than because she never seemed to doubt herself, and it was hard for him to take that in whole, her blazing certainties were too much for him. But what she told him on the long-distance line, taken even tricklingly, was difficult to ignore. "Some people are saying—do you know what they are *saying*?" She sobbed. "I've heard them say he was gay so he must have been crazy, as if gay people are just all completely crazy, and kill themselves for no reason—and they say he must have had HIV, and that must be why he did it, as if it isn't *perfectly obvious* what actually—it's so *hateful*—

and even if he *did*—oh God, they are such bastards. It makes me so angry I am *shaking*. I'm so sorry, Brian."

He thought he appreciated being told this, but he wasn't sure. As a conscript, he had declined to participate in speculation in the barracks about the sexuality of those unfortunates who were singled out for any of a number of failings—slight frames or fine gestures, a certain set of mouth perhaps, an unacceptably high voice. He'd kept out of it partly because he'd felt sorry for those guys, but also because the concept of gayness seemed at once both dirty and esoteric: a sleazy fog of compulsion, anuses, shit, cocks (too many cocks), self-absorption, and, yes, insanity and AIDS. Unnecessary and unhealthy to dwell upon. Alone in his room, Brian did not connect these notions to Andrew or his picture: but he felt them floating, now—in this torn and sticky web of people, tugging and twitching around him—just out of sight.

No one else spoke directly to his anxiety until the second evening of the wake, when Auntie Poh Lian and Uncle Bernard arrived in their gleaming grey Mercedes Benz. (The 1990s had been kind to the Lows.) Brian was having a smoke in the fading light at the edge of the car park when he saw them pull up. Four doors opened together, like the shuttering wings of an enormous metal beetle, and then thudded closed behind the emergent passengers, with a smooth and expensive weightiness.

He ground his cigarette with the toe of his sandal as the family advanced. "Auntie. Uncle." Poh Lian and Bernard acknowledged him with small nods and made their way over to his parents, leaving Brian alone with his cousins.

They stood together in an irregular triangle. Mabel, now twenty-four, still almost ascetically thin, was elegantly suited from another day in the office. She wore crisp make-up, a well-fitted silk shirt in baby blue, and a single pearl on a sleek gold chain. Jasmine, in an oversized muddy-orange T-shirt and faded bermudas, slouched a half-step behind, her gaze falling in corners and studiedly vague middle distances. She was clearly delegating all responsibility for human interaction to her older sister; who, for her part, regarded Brian owlishly, without speaking.

An unusually short interval had passed since he'd last seen them, at the Chinese New Year visits six weeks ago. They had exchanged the obligatory greetings, and then sat cracking open melon seed after melon seed, and picking at the fiddly white pith of mandarin peels, to pass the stilted hour while their parents conversed. Brian particularly liked the soft, melting kueh bankit, but there was only so much silence one could fill by eating, and only so much eating one could do, before even those feathery coconut cookies brought on a sense of sticky overfullness. The families rarely gathered for any other occasion now: Wa Ma, dead some three years, no longer required birthday celebrations with her children and grandchildren. Even at those dinners, the women and children had often been sequestered off at a different table, while Brian and Andrew, once they reached sixteen, had been seated with the men. So Brian had barely spoken to his cousins for years now, and possessed only skeletal notions of them—a satiny whiff of Mabel's careful grooming, a hint of Jasmine's negative intensity, and a dim feeling that the older sister had an obscure childhood reason for not liking him. He believed Mabel was an accountant somewhere in a big multinational firm, and that Jasmine was on a communications course at a polytechnic, but he wasn't sure that even these scraps of knowledge didn't come filtered through his mother, rather than from direct conversation.

"Hi," he said eventually.

"Sorry to hear about Andrew." The sentence began with Mabel and ended in a quiet, trailing echo from Jasmine.

"Thanks," he said, almost automatically. "Thanks for coming."

"I'm not sure when I last saw him, actually," Mabel said. "I think he hasn't been at Chinese New Year for a few years already. Since going to Cambridge."

"Yah," Brian said. "It was always during his term time. I also haven't seen him since last year, he came back for summer, then he went back for his Masters."

There was a pause, and then they spoke at the same time:

"Do you want to see his—"

"Did you know already about—"

They both stopped. After a confused moment Mabel went on.

"Did you know already he was a homosexual?" Like many Singaporeans she elongated the word, with equal, and heavy, emphasis on each syllable: *hoh-moh-seck-shuerl*. "Your mum told my mum about the photo," she continued, as Brian opened his mouth and then shut it again. "She was very upset, she thought maybe it is her fault. Was it a big shock to you also?"

"I don't want—I'm not—" Brian began, and then stopped, baffled. He looked to Jasmine for help, but she had, without moving, retreated even further away. Her face was firmly neutral, her eyes fixed on the pair of lizards resting on a nearby pillar. This pose was the result of meticulous craft: she had spent the day assiduously gathering her energies, so as to give this exact response at this precise moment. Appraised the night before of Mabel's intentions, she had keenly felt their crassness, and the danger to herself: the mortification, the vulgarity, the threat of conflict. "Eh, I think it's maybe not so nice to say leh," she had hazarded, without much hope. "People's brother just died, he won't be in the mood, and you know he isn't a Christian also, if you start talking about God he will just switch off lorh. It's not really our problem, don't so kaypoh, Mabel."

Her sister responded, implacably, with something about the importance of the Word, and being the salt and the light; and Jasmine, hearing this, gave up and reverted to her usual plan. She would erase herself, and ready her nerves for the trial of someone else's drama. She could not be blamed for just existing, or indeed for being present at her own cousin's wake; if she said and did nothing more, she would have no part of it; and when the whole sordid business was over, she would emerge cleanly and return to her tidy and tasteful life. With luck, this would take maybe twenty minutes of endurance. She was more than equal to that; she had perfected her powers of disconnect through countless slack-jawed hours, over many years, of family quarrels. Her mental space was a silent island of innocent neutrality, preserved amid the chaos of screams, blows and tears alike. When it came to handling confrontation, Jasmine was a dab hand.

So Brian was on his own. He turned back to Mabel, whose face was bright with expectation.

"Your mum was very worried she did something wrong. With your brother. To make him into a homosexual."

"I don't think we should talk about this."

"I know it's not very nice to bring it up, but it's important, I must tell you. I saw your mum; she was truly suffering. If we stay silent, never discuss about the problem, the suffering will be worse. Like my mum said to your mum, she must not blame herself. This homosexual behaviour, it was his choice to do it. And there is help for the homosexuals to become normal, but we must talk about it, otherwise they will not know what they are doing is wrong and they can change. My church has very good programmes, with experts from US—they have seen a lot of this kind of thing there, from their experience they know a lot about the homosexuals, they can tell you what to do. Andrew had this problem, but nobody to help—"

"No—you don't—that's not—he wasn't—" He stopped. He couldn't say what Andrew had or hadn't been: he had no idea. He had only the picture, and whatever it did or didn't mean, when he thought of the picture, and Andrew smiling from it, what Mabel was saying felt wrong. He tried again—"Andrew didn't have a problem,"—and regretted this instantly; it was a stupid thing to say; there was a body in a coffin a few metres away, which made that much clear. And now Mabel's face filled with a dreadful pity.

"Look," he said. "Whatever it is, okay, he's already, Andrew is dead already. So it doesn't matter, okay? Please, just, leave this, it, him, in peace."

"Your parents are very upset by this," Mabel said. "I think if it is my son, this thing is worse than him dying! God gave us more than this world and this life, but now it is not only Andrew's body that is dead, but his soul is lost to Christ forever, why? Because he went down this path, and this path is not just against the law, but a path of sin, and so he did not know that God loves him—"

"Please, Mabel," Brian said. "All this—church—stuff—"

He waved his hand. "It's got nothing to do with Andrew."

"Yah, that is what I am trying to tell you!" Mabel said impatiently. "He had a problem and God could have helped him. If only he accepted the Lord, but he pushed the Lord away, and embraced a homosexual lifestyle."

Brian's face flushed. "Please, Mabel, he is dead, whatever he did last time, whatever lifestyle—" (the word stung) "—or what—why do you want to bring it up, now it is—he is dead, how many times must I say?" Until now he had held back from a certain boundary, but now anger made him rash, propelled him over: "And if it made him happy, why do you care? Now he is dead—at least, let him be happy, at least he was happy, at least a little while."

Mabel gave a brusque shake of her head. "You don't know anything about this, Brian, I read up on it, the experts from US said before, the homosexuals think this lifestyle is what they want, and they become—" She paused to recall the words. "—they become *enslaved to a lie*, they think it makes them happy only, but they cannot see the truth. It leads to all kinds of negative things—usually AIDS lah, drugs lah—but even where that kind of thing don't have, homosexuality makes people turn away from their family, from God. They say, right, it makes them despair—that is why—we all know this is why he killed himself, Brian, over this homosexual problem."

Her voice rose here, to shut out his angry groan. "You

know it's true. Don't lie to yourself also. You better not make this same mistake with values. I only say for your own good. If you know anyone else with this homosexual problem, or if *you* have a problem—" (she held a hand up against his protests) "—any kind of problem, you should remember there is always help if you ask God. Always. No such thing as something He cannot solve." She looked at him significantly, and then, duty done, walked off to join her parents. Jasmine stood, still slumped, for a fraction of a second more, and then roused herself to follow. As far as she was concerned, it had all gone swimmingly; it was over, she noted, in record time.

For Mabel, the news about Andrew was touched with a kind of Providence. For a long time she had paid the whole gay thing, like all dirty things, little mind. It was only an occasional theme in church, after all, and she had reassured herself, early on, against a checklist of warning signs. Not just obvious ones, like inappropriate daydreams, but also subtler things, like being a tomboy. She knew she had come late to a proper attentiveness to femininity and its labyrinthine requirements as to appearance and demeanour. Now it had become a practised routine—finished nails, shaped eyebrows, restrained steps enforced by dainty shoes; and though she struggled, still, from time to time, with the prideful sense that this relegated her to a certain triviality, on the whole, she felt in no personal danger.

This complacency ended with the disgrace of a fellow leader in her church youth group. Competing accounts of his offence circulated among the congregation with perhaps less than Christlike glee. The more salacious concerned a Bible camp in the swamps of Pulau Ubin, a witching hour tryst, another boy blundering sleepily into the tent during the unspeakable act. Pastor Hong made no allusion to this idle gossip when he gathered the group leaders for a hushed and icy conference in the church's office. But even at their driest, the admitted facts—sexual misconduct, with a fifteen-year-old in the church's care—were scandalous enough.

Under thick blasts of air-conditioning, the pastor delivered a penitent lecture, touching on the gravity of this sin, the threat it posed to the integrity of the church, and his own shame at being deceived by this seemingly clean-cut young man. He vowed zero tolerance for such perversion amongst those tasked with spiritual leadership. They could not, of course, involve the secular authorities—that would only give ammunition to the enemies of Christ, who were multiplying in these increasingly Godless times. They must themselves be vigilant; the responsibility for rooting out the serpent lay with them all. Danger stalked, all around, in the most unlikely of places, and failure to act was itself culpable.

At this point of her life, Mabel thought of herself as having "calmed down". She looked back on early adolescence, with some indulgence, as a time when she had been moved to organise everyone and everything, to rankle against all injustice and iniquity, in the name of the Lord. She believed she had grown up since, directing the once tumultuous stream of her faith into the smoother plains of the church's organisation; and also acquiring the steadying accoutrements of status, both professional and social: the practical degree, the good job, the respectable churchgoing boyfriend. (These things seemed also to propitiate her mother. At any rate she was no longer beaten.) Glossiness and also godliness: perhaps life was not after all so inhospitable to the righteous.

But this disgrace, and those strong words from the pastor she so admired—these things unsettled her, and sparked something like her old sense of the world's fundamental hostility. She dug into some Christian resources on sexual deviance, and armed herself with knowledge. This seemed at first excessive caution: but two weeks later, on an overcast Saturday, God spoke. She unlocked the door to her home and found Auntie Poh Ling weeping at the dining table amongst tufts of crumpled, sodden tissue. Mabel's mother, vigorously stroking her sister's back, nodded grimly to Mabel, and gestured for her to make something to drink and sort the mess out.

Two cups sat where they were placed, cooling untouched through the afternoon: Poh Ling and Poh Lian were too busy with sobs, and speculations, and recriminations, for tea.

Mabel drank hers, Lipton with its grainy bitter aftertaste, and listened.

And what a tale. For years, Andrew had been a legend. There had been no end to the boasts and the praise, originating from his parents, absorbed and re-transmitted by hers. Poh Lian's hairdresser and Bernard's golf caddy had heard all about this boy, who was in not only Ashford Hall but also the Gifted Education Programme. (This crowning apex of the Singaporean taxonomy of young human capital devoted especial resources to only the brainiest half of a hundredth of children—though its strictly scientific process lighted remarkably often, statistically speaking, upon the affluent.) Bernard's siblings were duly informed when Andrew enrolled in the top junior college; and Poh Lian's mahjong kakis knew this nephew wasn't just a bookworm, but also captain of the school badminton team, and Vice President of the Student Council as well. By the time he appeared in the papers, little more had to be said: everyone saw immediately that Bernard and Poh Lian were bathed in the silver glory of this achievement, too.

And yet. Mabel was privy to remarks her parents made, in the confines of their home, about Poh Ling and Kim Seng: who lived in public housing, drove a small Malaysian car, enjoyed no memberships even in the cheapest country club, and were entirely ignorant about the higher callings of church life. They were socially backward; they didn't give their children proper guidance. Andrew was no credit to them—they were just lucky, he could as easily have been his brother, that boy, always daydreaming, no drive. And of course these exam results and scholarships were all very well and good, but it didn't mean Andrew could make it in the "real world", the one that had delivered the grey Mercedes. Nor did it mean he had the important things in life correct. Their own daughters might not be such academic high-flyers, but they were good Christians; and didn't that, in a way, matter more than mere grades? In fact, it was quite sad, quite meaningless, wasn't it, to have all these certificates and whatnot but not to know anything higher than this life, or to have the right values?

The last of these waves of judgment not only washed over Mabel, but left some of its grit behind. Apart from the spectacle of Andrew the achiever, full of worldly cleverness, she had long had another, lingering, sense—that her cousin could have been, if the chips had fallen differently, truly thoughtful. In him lurked the spiritual depth to appreciate the Almighty; it was only dry happenstance that he didn't. "Calmed down" Mabel felt the great and searing waste of this only latently, as the reflected ripples of a lost pebble, which had skimmed across a lake and sunk. But this impression was forcefully resurrected in the Mabel who witnessed the heartbreak of her aunt, over the son whose name had once been synonymous with every reason for pride. Now the gears and engines were exposed, and Andrew's rootlessness was revealed to be not merely banal anomaly, but tragedy. The surfaces of things really did hide malevolences. Mabel had to act.

Over in Simei, Lay Choo sat hunched on the sofa, staring at the condensation on the outside of her glass. A fine pinprick pattern appeared from the air on the pale amber frosting, and then the thin drops glommed together at irregular intervals, and ran to soak the cardboard coaster on her new coffee table. It irritated her. She did not move it.

"Why don't you just go?" Nurul's voice floated from the open kitchen door. A knife sounded steadily over a chopping block.

"Told you already, he said I better not go, it is shameful to the family, if I show my face there he will never call me sister any more, all that kind of thing. He said all of this is my fault, my bad influence, it is because of me his son is dead."

"Aiyah, how many times has he said this kind of drama things? Last time also, in the end also gostan, everything was okay."

"Yah, but now people's son, you know."

"End of the day also your nephew, you want to pay your respects, I'm sure he knows this is correct also. He just say only."

"Yah," Lay Choo said doubtfully. "But." She did not know how to divide it into closer parts, this lumpish mass of negation. The loss of Andrew had a distanced quality to it, for her; and this in itself felt, abstractly, wrong. She had ladled rice and soup for her nephew into many a bowl, but she could not say that she knew him much at all. In the early days she had tentatively imagined friendship with the children of her brothers and sisters, as they unfolded into people. They seemed natural allies when they were born—at thirteen, fifteen, sixteen, even eighteen, Lay Choo felt with these new faces a kindred incompleteness. But her life whirled quickly on into jobs and paperwork; and at family gatherings, their obedient silence as children grew seamlessly into the fierce reserve of teenagers. Whatever currents flickered in their hidden lives, they could not spark at the family dinner table. Kim Seng's sons were, for her, mediated by her brother's matrix of expectations—exam results, prizes, discipline and management—and they saw her, she knew, sitting across from them at the narrow table with its stiff chairs, as just another in a set of aunts, an accessory to their parents, irrelevantly there.

She might have submerged the uncertain mourning of Andrew for his own sake into mourning him for her brother's sake, but that wretched phone call forbade it. She struggled to tease apart the wrong done to her and the (surely much greater) wrong done to her nephew. She felt guilty about this running together of things. She felt angry about her guilt.

Glum silence gave way to the merciful scent and sizzle of onions. Lay Choo put her face in her hands, enveloping the clean walls of her home in the black warmth behind them. Long before she first set eyes on this flat (almost three years ago), or moved in (a few months later), all the lines of her life had run towards it, as towards a vanishing point on paper. The hope of this place had oriented almost every facet of her decisions and her doings. For her and Nurul merely to share a meal cooked in their own kitchen was a triumph; to wake up together each morning a luxury. After everything, it seemed terribly unfair that she could not, now, have peace.

Lay Choo had spent the better part of her twenties wishing her youth away. This wasn't so at first. For a few months after that sandy grey night, when she and Nurul sat on the breakwater and talked till dawn, fingers interlaced in the sunrise, she felt life fill with a rising tide. Nothing seemed more wonderful than that she should be so unmoored, that she could have washed into a world so vast and unknown in its joys as this. Things were finally beginning: after those suspended school days when she had permitted herself only glittery crushes on distant girls with wide eyes and sleek ponytails. Two seconds of caught breath as she passed them, moth-like, in the corridors. Pale-bright flares of excitement, from which no shadows could deepen. But then adulthood, and Nurul: it was as easy as growing. They had become immediately close; and then closer; and then everything had opened. If this could exist, and exist for her, then the worst and the hardest must be over. Every future moment must be a gift, a treasure to be savoured—

—ridiculous, to be sure, and sentimental, of course; but allow her this for now, because life's ugly muddle accretes around it soon enough. What began in delighted disbelief, sweet as air, thickened fiercely, developed forces and demands of its own. And started to feel crowded in. Lay Choo's mother didn't understand why her daughter had to shut her bedroom door, or why this friend had to disturb everyone by being in their flat until so late. Didn't she have a family of her own to stay with? To that family, then: the pair nestled down in Nurul's fusty small room with its narrow single bed, and the ratty old curtain always over the window. Her brother Imran was unconcerned. Outside, at all hours, his friends, too, came and went; there were footsteps and music, cigarette smoke and talk; and there was word of Imran's marriage plans and his new wife moving in.

Perhaps they should have explained themselves to him, negotiated a home out of this waystation. Imran and Norhaili might have said yes. Imran thought he understood the nature of his sister's friendship, but assumed she had her reasons for silence, and he was too delicate to ask. With the lofty clarity of the theorist, we can sketch them some happy orbits: four people in one apartment, tracing overlapping circles in peaceable parity. But Lay Choo and Nurul could not conceive of such an arrangement; it was too audacious, they had always needed walls to brick their secrets in, and they imagined that they always would. At a last ditch they could hire their walls by the hour in the hotels of Geylang and Balestier, among brothels and gambling houses, but despite its neatness and its safety, the succession of anonymous rental beds only left them feeling more adrift.

Lay Choo was frustrated. She could trim and squash and redact so much: she had never been interested in bridal fuss and frippery; in public, she kept her hands dutifully back from Nurul's waist; and except among a tiny knot of trusted friends, she skipped deftly over strategic gaps in her patter. But there was no arguing with the fundamental fact of bodies needing room: for movement, and for rest.

And so she sat down to work out the Byzantine rules governing sales and resales of HDB flats—the only housing option she and Nurul could ever afford—and determined that there was nothing else for it. She would have to turn thirty-five, and as soon as possible. The only alternative was hoping for her mother to die: an unacceptable position, and anyway unreliable. With five siblings and a troupe of nieces and nephews, she was unlikely to inherit the whole flat; and if she didn't, there remained Kim Hock to reckon with. Until he reached thirty-five (only eighteen months before she would) or married (halitosis notwithstanding), the rules might require them, as brother and sister, to make any flat purchases together.

So the waiting game began. She worked hard—was

promoted—duty manager, branch manager, Customer Relations in head office—eyes always on the prize. She had it all lined up—she would be ready—she *was* ready—she wanted to be older. She and Nurul continued to quilt their patchwork weeks together: the brief relief of afternoons crumpled and hastily pocketed; a few hours in a cinema like guilty teenagers; now and then a lucky find, an entire night. She kept a running tally in her head: this many more years in the decade, this many more months in the year. Every time she wrote a date she made a quick calculation of the time to go.

Their situation softened slightly. Lay Choo's old mother befriended Nurul, and enjoyed having her around, though this too had its bitterness. "Nurul," Ma lisped in Melayu. "You're a nice girl, you must have lots of friends, can't you introduce someone to my daughter? You should get her to wear clothes like yours also, much nicer, you see she is always dressed so sloppily. How will she find a husband?" Her views on the necessity of husbands were robust: they had survived the nation's independence from the British Empire, its ejection from the Federation of Malaysia, the cot death of its democracy, the destruction of its kampung villages, and perhaps most impressively, her own husband, with his liver cirrhosis and his liberal fists. They would survive a lesbian daughter.

It was having Nurul about so much that prompted a question from Kim Seng.

"Your friend, this Nurul," he began. "I noticed she always come here. You sure she is not disturbing Ma?"

He was sitting at the kitchen table. It was a Saturday morning and he had come over for lunch. Kim Hock and their mother were in the living room watching a game show on the television. Every now and then muffled laughter or applause reached the pair in the kitchen, over the low murmur of rain.

"No," Lay Choo said lightly. "I got ask Ma before, she said she doesn't mind." She bent a little further over the bin, keeping up a constant rhythm of peeler against potato.

"Hrm. Okay, good that you asked her." He looked out of the window, picking absent-mindedly at a thickened patch of skin on the bottom of his foot. "She argues a lot with her parents, is it, this Nurul?"

"No," Lay Choo said. "Think I got tell you before, her father and mother died long time ago. Car accident."

"Is it? Then she lives with who?"

"Brother. She got one older brother, he drives taxi."

"She doesn't get on with him?"

"No lah, why you say that?" Lay Choo said. "Think they are okay." She brought the skinned potatoes to the stove, and turned her back to him with deliberate slowness. Where were these questions going?

"Hrm. I see. And no boyfriend?"

"No." Surely he had not guessed? She and Nurul had been together three years now, and she generally had little difficulty hiding the truth. In her school days her classmates had taken her careless rhapsodies on her crushes as the rightful abasement of one schoolgirl before the enviable prettiness of others. "Lesbian" was only an outrageous punchline, a self-evident absurdity; she had merely to laugh along at it, and all was forgiven. It might be whispered semi-seriously as a criticism of the tanned, broad-shouldered giants of the basketball team, but not of Lay Choo, with her abundant hair and her birdlike air. When it came to women, she found, most people had astonishingly limited minds. They took for granted that she wanted to *look like* something; they could not imagine she ached to *touch* someone. And much as she liked Kim Seng, she did not think he was capable of any more than others on this score. She wondered if her brief answers were not as casual as she hoped—perhaps she should say more.

"I am just wondering," her brother continued, "why she is always here. I think it is not very healthy, she should be with her own family, or find someone settle down, or with some Malay friends, don't see why she is whole day here disturbing. Don't know if she is trying some kind of funny business or what."

"Aiyoh, say until so suspicious like that! You think what, Hong Kong drama serial ah? We are all big businessmen, some kind of towkay family, and she wants to steal our secrets? Xiao." She made herself turn to him then, with a wide, automatic smile. "People friend mah. Like to watch the same movies, talk about the same things. Ma likes her also. She cooks dinner for us sometimes. Her nasi bryani very good, okay. Next time I ask her to make for you also lah. Eat already won't say this kind of crazy things."

It worked, as usual. Kim Seng continued to pick at the skin on his foot, the potatoes found their place in a chicken curry, and nothing more was said. But that evening, sitting with Nurul in the smoke and bustle of the hawker centre, Lay Choo became pensive. It was so easy to lie. Had she grown too used to jesting and simpering her way around the plain facts of her life? There were gaps between her and this favourite brother, but she had always looked up to him, perhaps because she had been quite so small when their father finally sank beneath the stout and the lager, and Ma had gone to pieces for a time. She remembered being seven years old, and Kim Seng finding her after twenty minutes' panic in the snaking warren of a building site. He had surprised her by scooping her to him, and making no reproach. And, once, when she had washed into hot tears over a quarrel at school, he had unbent from his habitual stiffness to pat her awkwardly, and bring her some kueh. When he came by, he sat and talked with her in the kitchen precisely because he liked her. He liked her. That must count for something; she couldn't be sure that he was safe, but mightn't she hope that he would try?

Nurul took off her glasses and rubbed her eyes. She was sceptical. She had noticed Kim Seng's unsmiling stares. His astringent remarks on his sister Lay Peng's ongoing divorce and on the multiplying rolls of flesh on her belly (subjects that seemed for him mysteriously connected) did not inspire confidence in his powers of sympathy. She would never dream of making confessions to her own brother without something stronger to go on. But then Imran had never asked; and every family was different; and really, she couldn't bring herself to be too discouraging to this oddly torn version of Lay Choo, who spoke in pleading bursts, and whose hands agitated in hopeless, involved circles, while her mee goreng went cold on its plate.

"I don't know," Nurul said at last. "Really, Choo, actually, what I see so far, I don't think he will be okay with it. But I only met him so few times, he is your brother, you know him better." She paused. "Will he tell other people? If he won't, then worst case is just he himself is angry, right?" She reached out to brush Lay Choo's hand briefly, and was gratified to see the defeat lift for a moment from those soft eyes.

Lay Choo started the search with the sleeper's maddening certainty of something half imagined, half remembered: if the method could only be found, the rest would follow in perfect order. And so they play-acted. They made, and ripped up, careful plans. They grappled wordily over tactical details. His place or hers? Should they both be there? How to get him away from Poh Ling? Or might she be a calming influence? Nurul began to suspect it was like cracking an egg: the angle of attack could make no difference, it all came in the end to the same sticky spillage. No decision was made, no strategy was formulated, and she wasn't entirely surprised when Lay Choo called her one day to say that she had simply blurted the lot out, and it had been a disaster.

Lay Choo could not find the energy to blame herself for playing it wrongly. Merely conveying the basic facts to Kim Seng turned out to be mind-bendingly difficult. Confusion pinched her brother's face. What did she mean, she and Nurul were "more than friends"? No matter how good her friends, at some point she had to find a husband and settle down. How could she "settle down with Nurul"? They could not be "like married to each other"—did she even understand, in the first place, what married couples did? It didn't make sense to say that about two women. What kind of rubbish was she talking?

Lay Choo fell into an angry and embarrassed silence at the patronising stupidity of this. Did she honestly have to explain to him that you didn't need a cock to do it? This was not what she had wanted to talk about. It was nothing, she muttered, it had been a mistake, she tried to take it back, but he seemed suddenly, cheeks reddening, to comprehend well enough. This was some kind of dirty sexy business she had been taught by a perverted Malay. How could Lay Choo be so shameless, doing this kind of disgusting thing, and then telling her brother about it? They had failed to bring her up properly, he and Ma, she would break Ma's heart, she would kill Ma with her selfishness. His voice rose in horror as it occurred to him—Lay Choo had even brought this woman into Ma's home to take part in this sick nonsense. What if she tried anything funny with Ma? Lay Choo was an ingrate. She should not call herself a Teo.

So be it, she decided, and walked away. It was all so miserably predictable in hindsight. She told Nurul that his disapproval was too stupid to get upset about, and it followed that his approval was not worth seeking. She had lost nothing but a lie, the lie that he had ever really cared for her. Pining after it would only be weakness. She told Nurul this, and she believed it, too, or felt that she should: neatly defining the ragged ache in her chest out of existence.

She had barely replaced the receiver when Kim Seng himself telephoned to elaborate upon her defects. She must end this disgraceful behaviour now. How would she have children? She wouldn't, she replied coolly. Every woman wanted children: she would regret this. She didn't think so. Had she bothered to consider that Ma wanted grandchildren? She pointed out that Ma already had grandchildren. He lost any veneer of patience. How could she choose this perverted Malay woman over her own brother? She was letting the family down. She hung up on him.

Life went on. Kim Seng spoke only to Kim Hock and Ma, ignoring his sister, when he turned up at the flat. They did not notice. Ma had a small fall, and some trouble walking for a while. She mentioned, as they sat around the lunch table, layering sweet sauces, stewed turnips and ground peanuts into the fresh thin skin of popiah rolls, that that nice Nurul girl had been very good to her that week, helping her to get around. Her son compressed his lips into a thin line, and changed the subject. During each visit, Lay Choo was studiously cold; and if she once or twice sat in her room, crying, after her brother and his prejudices had left, she did not admit such anomalous acts of unreason even to herself.

Five months later, without warning, he came into the kitchen, as of old. He spoke without looking directly at Lay Choo, appearing instead to study the calendar hanging by her head.

"Your this Nurul business."

"What?" She was surprised into turning to him.

"Your this Nurul business," he repeated. "You know already lah, I think it is not good for you, but—" (he gestured a quick plea for attention, as she began to roll her eyes) "—you are an adult, yah, you want to get yourself involved in this kind of thing, it is your own business, your own problem. But you must remember, no matter what, what you get up to with what other people, you must think about your family. So—you better not anyhow say what, you and this Nurul are more than friends or what, all over the place, later Ma hear about it, then you know. This kind of thing, hear already you will make her very unhappy. I also don't want to hear about it from other people." He paused and ended grudgingly, "Don't go and tell outsiders and make trouble for Ma, can already."

It was as close to reconciliatory language as she was going to get. A tightness in her throat eased. (She hadn't realised she was carrying it.) She missed something about the clarity of rage, though, because it was difficult, being alive to his opinions or his silences again, and feeling the absence, like a phantom limb, of something more which she had once thought connected them.

Yet there was a happy ending. It began, unexpectedly, on a Saturday, in the supermarket aisle between the rows of instant noodles and the bottles of sauces and marinades. There Lay Choo lowered her basket to the floor for a moment, winded by a sudden throbbing flare in her belly. All morning her body had pulled dully at her from the inside, and now it gave a sharper, more insistent yank. She bent over to collect herself, but before she could go on, a second round fired, and a third, and then they smeared into a blur of pain. She was on her knees, her mouth hot with the afterburn of vomit, as her mother rushed over from the next aisle to her side.

Somehow they got into a taxi. The journey washed by in agony. The pain had an alarming grip: it crested and surged, and after each momentary slackening seemed only to dig deeper. Thought was impossible—everything shrank into, was swallowed up by, this clawing and scraping inside. But Ma surprised Lay Choo with her calm: she spoke only sparingly, and gently, but kept a steady pressure on her daughter's hand: and the dual focal points of pressure and surprise kept Lay Choo from dissolving into panic.

At the hospital there were doctors and questions and prodding and needles, and eventually she was told that it was appendicitis. They would have to operate. As she hadn't eaten since breakfast, she could have the slot that was open that evening. She lay in an immobile haze—pain was, who would have thought, really rather exhausting—and worried, through it, about Nurul. Dared she ask Ma to make a phone call? Some facile pretext or another, they were meant to meet that day and she didn't want to leave a friend waiting… Nurul would know how to manage her reactions, not to give the game away. The nurses approached her bed with painkillers.

By the time Ma returned from the toilet, Lay Choo had been swept into a cloudlike chemical blank, Nurul forgotten.

The happy ending comes the next morning, several hours after Lay Choo first awakes, one appendix down, and she is at last deemed ready for visitors. Clutching a few wet flower stalks, her face arranged into perfect shades of concern, relief and delight, Nurul walks in, perhaps leading Ma and Kim Seng or perhaps behind them—Lay Choo can't track such details, she is too floodlit with joy at the sight of those beloved hands, shoulders, face.

So, it seemed, Kim Seng had looked—with what inner struggles only he can know—into the slim black book of numbers by the telephone. No matter that the nurse came in to chide them about crowding the room, so that Nurul stepped out for appearance's sake. No matter that Kim Seng never did warm to Nurul afterward, and always spoke of her as at a distance. No matter that during the visits that Lay Choo began, once more, to make, her brother would sometimes, in fact rather too often, pose annoying questions about when Lay Choo might find a boyfriend, or if she still ate pork. She brushed this detritus aside: Kim Seng had thought to make this one phone call, and that was for Lay Choo the proof she needed. When serious matters were in the balance, he would be on her side. For her, this was a promise of future victory.

And her home, here and now, was full of yellow evening light and the warbling of birds congregating in the hash of crossing branches outside. It felt like ingratitude, to whom she couldn't say, to possess all of this and yet to feel dejected on her own account. She had this haven now, a little safe sleep: could she really need more? A chubby wooden hippopotamus gawped at her from the television stand across the room. Kim Seng had helped with boxes on the day she moved in—she had a memory of him paused right there, mopping trails of sweat from his brow.

"Choo, dinner."

The food was fresh, sharp, good. A few hot mouthfuls and her plate was clean. She was surprised by her own appetite, and then troubled. Her nephew was dead, and she was eating. He had been alive, and she had done nothing.

"I wish," she started, putting her spoon down.

"Yah?"

"What Seng said, it's so stupid. What bad influence, I am the one who killed his son and all that."

"Yah, of course. Please, Choo, don't listen to his…you never even said one word to Andrew about you and me. And even if you said, so what? You are you, he is him, we are nothing to do with him and what happened. Your brother is just being unreasonable. Again."

"Yah, I know, but, you know, right, I do feel bad—I feel like it's my fault, *not*—" (she held her hands up against Nurul's astonishment) "—not like Seng said, but something like the opposite. I feel like actually I should have told Andrew about us, like maybe if he knew, it would have helped him." She gestured around her. "If he knew it could be okay."

"Maybe. But you didn't know about him…"

"No. And if I told him and Seng found out…"

"Yah, then you would really get it from him." Nurul gave a small, bitter laugh. "But then now you are getting it anyway."

It was very quiet now, except for the hum of the ceiling fan and the faint whine of cicadas. The chorus of birdsong had gone out.

"I don't know. Maybe telling him would also be no use. Don't even know why he did it in the end."

"No."

"But I still feel like I wish I told him. Don't care how angry Seng would be. And maybe Andrew had don't know what other problems, but at least then he could have some kind of, I don't know, he could have seen a future. I should have told him. I should go now and tell his brother. And Peng's kids and Teng's and Guan's also. Someone should tell them. Just in case. Just tell them, it can be okay."

Nurul crossed the small space between them, and they held each other for a long time: Lay Choo flushed with longing and resolve, with the sense of opportunities missed.

But later, turning and turning again in the dark, sleep hopelessly far off, she thought: she would not say anything to anyone. There was really nothing to say. In the grey of those small hours the room filled with the white noise of Kim Seng's rage. The same words again on the telephone line: sick, disgusting, perverted, selfish, sick, ungrateful. They were ugly words, empty, so far beneath her, so unworthy of this space. And yet indissoluble: they were again and after so long still her companions. No walls, it seemed, could keep them out. Lay Choo touched Nurul's arm: her lover shifted and subsided, and breathed evenly by her side: and if even this certainty, this joy, could not keep her safe, if she could not even protect herself, she thought, what magic words could she ever have uttered against the long night Andrew had known?

# JANUARY 1993

I T WAS DARK out when Andrew woke up on the battered old cane couch in the Student Council room. He sat up quickly, a little confused. A fellow councillor was laughing at him from across the room. "Hey, hey! I didn't know should I wake you up or not, you were sleeping until so peaceful like that!"

"What time is it?"

"Almost eight already. I think everyone else went home already. Sorry Andrew, my mother is coming to pick me up, I can't walk to bus stop with you."

"It's okay."

"See you tomorrow," she sang out as she left, soft bag slung over one shoulder.

Andrew ran a hand through his hair and tried to smooth his rumpled uniform. A triangle of white shirt had escaped from the waistband of his trousers. He wasn't normally one for naps, but the last few days had tired him out. He was glad that the school would be empty. His group of newly arrived Year Ones seemed to be enjoying Orientation—the trust falls, the mass dances, the treasure hunts—but his own attention was absorbed in bustle and logistics, in the job of shepherding them around, and he felt himself to be observing, rather than experiencing, the atmosphere of fun. He couldn't quite remember how it had been on his turn, last year.

He was privately eager for the introductory week to end and for proper lessons to start, so that he could return to the genuine interest of their ideas, his work.

The lure of this was stronger now than ever. Stitched tightly into the pleasure of work was also its promise, and that promise had always been this next step, after this final year of school: university. Enter the right one and membership in the world was assured; fail and shadow foreclosed on every future possibility. You could still do things without a good degree, of course—even, to be thoroughly logical, without a degree at all—but not things that counted. This was his primly abstracted version of the parental admonition repeated throughout his childhood: "Must work hard, otherwise next time become roadsweeper, then you know!" Real people did not sweep roads. That the roads were nevertheless swept, and presumably by someone, had no bearing on this axiom.

This future had taken on new urgency since last July, when he had been flown to Moscow for the International Mathematical Olympiad.

"The *what*?" Ming Wei had asked.

"It's a really big maths competition. People come from

schools from lots of different countries and solve problems."

"What—I can't imagine anything sadder. I mean, good for you lah, you just happen to be a genius, but the other people must be the biggest nerds in the world."

After returning, Andrew struggled to correct this description. "A really big maths competition", populated by "the biggest nerds in the world", was accurate enough. But it gave no indication of how the two short weeks had changed everything for him.

He hadn't expected this, before the trip. He hadn't had expectations at all. Oddly perhaps for a boy who'd never been further from home than a three-hour bus ride, he had not felt the glamour of international flight. He could not have conceived of Moscow, so immense and so alien, any more than of Mars. His only real feeling prior to the journey had been relief, relief that he had done well enough to be selected for the team. Even on the day of departure, the mechanics of travel seemed terribly unexciting, as he wrestled at the Changi check-in counter with a creaky old suitcase, stashed with too-big woolly jumpers borrowed from Uncle Bernard.

But when it came, it came all at once, like a plunge into a cold bath. Sheremetyevo Airport alone was full of bewildering things: Cyrillic script; the heavy blond stare and thick accent of the immigration official; the impossible pleasure, for an equatorial child, of cool outdoor sunshine, as the chaperone from the Ministry of Education herded the team toward the tournament bus. The bus itself was foreign smelling, from old upholstery, and already full of hopeful teenagers from places Andrew was unable to picture even theoretically. People of ethnicities he couldn't guess at to name. Across the aisle a smiling, dark-eyed Argentinian boy said "*Hola*," and Andrew was dazzled.

The stream of sensation might have become too much, but once the maths arrived, he began to be able to order and manage strands of everything. The problems gave him focus. He could see that they were built up, at bottom, of parts he understood, though he had to shift into high gear to approach anything like the neighbourhood of solutions. Maths also lessened the total mystery of the other participants: talk emerged, frail but real, from its thin threads of commonality. Andrew worked for every word. He was elated by the smallest exchanges of sense in the most halting English. He felt continually sharpened, like a pencil.

The team didn't place well, but to his surprise, Andrew didn't much care. He realised early on that he was out of his league, maths-wise. What troubled him during the long flight home, as he shifted and turned in the cramped and scratchy airplane seat, was that the world had already shrunk rapidly, into this dark cabin and its stale air, and was hurtling back through the clouds, further and further from the crackling magic, the continents of novelty, of the last few hectic days.

The idea came to him, and immediately gathered

irresistible force, that in Moscow he had tasted a tiny silver slice of the future, his future, lying just around the corner. For the first time, it occurred to him that university would involve not just consequences and qualifications, but beautiful problems yet to be explored, and conversations yet to be created, with people yet to be met. Before he received any degrees, he would linger a while in college quadrangles: and now that he saw these waiting phantom spaces, however faintly, they threw ambient shadows and reflections over the complexion of the present.

School became boring. He was coasting, dotting and crossing what was put in front of him. Treading the flat grass flatter. He had always done this, but he had never noticed the tedium of it before. (How could he? The world celebrated him for it.) He felt impatient with this stage of things, and at the same time distrustful of his own impatience. These were necessary steps, after all. It was part of the way ahead. There was no point in resenting what had to be done; it was like protesting gravity, it made you careless. He was doing well, there was a plan, he shouldn't mess with it. He promised himself he wouldn't mess with it.

"Hello?"

A blurred figure hovered in the doorway, resolving into an uncertain-looking boy in a uniform Andrew didn't recognise. Green trousers and green collar on white shirt. A Year One, then, but not one of the group Andrew was in charge of—

he'd diligently learned all their names and faces.

"You're not supposed to be in here," he said automatically, sitting up straighter. "It's for councillors only."

"I know," the boy said. He hesitated on the threshold for a moment, and then came in, and began to talk at length, while gesturing vaguely in front of himself. "But I wanted to talk to you. You're Andrew, right? I hope it's not weird I know your name, but I guess you're used to it, right? You guys are up there on stage in front every day, so of course we all know you. Anyway, we talked the other day—remember? At the track there. I wasn't in uniform that time, I was wearing PE shorts, I was sitting down and you talked to me. I didn't say my name, it's Kevin—Kevin Cheng—it was the second day, Tuesday—okay, I can tell you don't remember."

He deflated a little, and at this Andrew placed him, dimly. "No, I think I remember." There had been a boy, at some point, it was true, with a flushed, sweaty face, his mouth twisted in unhappiness, grass caught in rogue tufts of his hair. They'd exchanged a few words, the gist being that the boy—Kevin—was in fact okay, and Andrew had hurried on to the next set of icebreaker games on his schedule.

"Oh, you do!"

"I think so. So what question did you have?"

"It's not really a question." He slipped around the large meeting table and pulled up a grey chair in which to sit himself, about a metre from Andrew. He was a broad-shouldered boy, but thin, with narrow hips. He leaned forward eagerly. "It's more I wanted to talk to you about—about Orientation—we feel very uncomfortable with a lot of things—we—that's me and Leila, she's also in my group—we had this idea we could talk to you about it. Or I did, anyway, Leila thought there was no point, but I told her about how you talked to me, and I thought you would listen."

Andrew put a careful hand to his chin. He wasn't sure what was going on, but he gathered this was the sort of thing he had heard teachers describe, summatively, as "pastoral care". People with problems, basically. Neither he nor his friends ever had anything to do with it. "Which group are you in?" he asked.

"What? Oh—Panther."

"That's John Almeida and Sangeetha's group, isn't it? Did you talk to them?"

"No," Kevin said quickly. "Of course not! That would defeat the—they're the ones who—sorry, I'm not making sense. I'll start again. That day when you talked to me, I was—not happy—because—they—the group—and John—they tau pokked me, and I really don't want to be tau pokked. I know—" He waved his palms at Andrew, to forestall a response. "I know that's the whole point, everybody says no, but I *really don't want it.*"

Andrew wasn't sure what he had expected Kevin to bring up: but not this, anyway. Tau pok was a beloved school tradition, a particular staple during Orientation Week, but popular all year round. One boy was pushed to the ground (girls were exempt, by unspoken convention), where he lay, stomach-down, while other students piled upon him, with lots of hooting and gasping, to form a heaving stack, six or seven bodies high.

"Is it really so bad?" he asked. "Everyone seems to enjoy it."

Kevin gave him a sceptical look. "You've never been on the bottom before, right?" Andrew shook his head. "It's horrible, they crush you—the weight is so enormous, you feel like your ribs will break—and you can't breathe, and you can't fight back, and you don't know if it will ever end. It's like—it's like being beaten up, and in the meantime they're all laughing and enjoying themselves, like everyone is celebrating beating you up."

This seemed much too dramatic a response to an ordinary, even a festive, activity. "They don't mean it to be mean," Andrew said without thinking. "It's just a joke."

"That doesn't make it *better*," Kevin said. "I'm in pain and they find it *funny*—how is it any better that they think beating me up is *entertaining*?"

Andrew felt suddenly that his own remarks had been feeble, even insulting, and stopped himself from asking the next question that rose in him. Of course it would have made no difference if Kevin had said anything to the group. Protests from the tau pok's bottom layer were always ignored:

they were, by definition, part of the game. That was the fun, the spirit, of the thing—not this fierce, wounded gaze from this highly-strung boy.

Out the window, the field was a wash of insect sound. After a few moments, Andrew turned back to Kevin. "Yeah, okay. That is bad." The other boy visibly brightened. "And—" Andrew hesitated. "Maybe you could talk to John and Sangeetha—or just Sangeetha, might be better—another time. When it's quiet lah, not just before another tau pok. If you want them to stop, I think they will listen more if you do that."

Kevin shook his head. "The tau pok is only one example. It's more than that. It's everything. The entire introduction we've had to this school." His voice grew somehow both bolder and more nervous at the same time. He always let himself down at these critical moments, he felt: the words that would make everything clear racing upstream in perfect formation and then collapsing, jumbled, in retreat, in the air. "It's a whole—soup—of everything. They made us do this—thing—we had to pair up, the girls had to lie down and the guys had to do push-ups over them." He felt stupid just describing it. "And another group tied this girl to the car park railing and threw buckets of water over her. She was screaming and crying and they just went on, like it was hilarious." He paused. "Why do you guys do this? It's like the whole point of the things you do is to make us feel dumb."

The last stung. "It's not meant like that," Andrew said. "It's just for bonding. I heard about that girl, later she said she really enjoyed it. It brings the groups together. It's just fun."

"But it's not!" Kevin half-shouted. "It's just not! We said we didn't want to, and they spent ten minutes—*ten minutes*—trying to make Leila and me do the push-ups. They surrounded us and kept on saying we had to. They didn't stop, they wouldn't go away, until we gave in and did the start position for them. How is that fun for anyone?" He blinked back tears. "Why is it fun to make people do things they don't want to? If forcing people to do things—and making them force other people to do things—if that is really what bonding means, that's horrible. It's stupid, and, and it's wrong. Why would you want to make a school like that?"

Andrew was annoyed. It wasn't as if he adored every last Orientation activity either. Was a little push-up so great a price for social passage? Kevin could just learn to roll with it, as they all did, without quite so much yelling and crying. On the other hand, the yelling and crying were a large part of the exasperating justice of Kevin's argument—and Andrew did, if he was honest, see that it was justice. There was no harm in it if this boy and his friend simply wanted to be left alone; and there was something awful, something chilling, in this vision of badgering and cajoling.

"Okay," he said. "You have a point."

"I really hoped you would get it."

"I think probably the group handled things badly."

"It's not just handling," Kevin said. "It's the...the problem is in what they have to handle. They should just stop having this whole stupid Orientation in this way. It's—it's poisonous. It's built around nastiness."

"You can't say that. A lot of people find it fun."

"But they shouldn't!"

Andrew frowned. "Don't you think you're going a bit far now? Okay, you don't want to take part, fine, nobody should force you. But most people like it."

"Most people *have to* like it!" Kevin was shouting again. "They have no choice! Because they know they're supposed to just *get over it*. Everyone has to show how *sporting* they are—nobody wants to become the cry baby—nobody wants to end up like me."

Andrew closed his eyes. He didn't want to agree with this; it was, he realised, conceding the case. It was frustrating. How had Kevin managed to turn his own weakness into a winning salvo? But the magnitude of his complaint was impossible. He might sneak it into the Council room on one unusually quiet night, but once exposed to the ordinary flow of discussion, the momentum of how the student body did things, it would soon be swept downstream like so much detritus. It wouldn't last a second in the sunlight of inspection by the others. Surely Kevin knew this, too: so why was he bothering Andrew?

"Look, I'm sorry you didn't enjoy yourself, but it's almost over. Tomorrow is the last day already. There's really no point telling me about this." The last came out a little more aggressively than he'd meant it to. He stood up and reached for his rucksack, which lay at the end of the couch.

"I just thought you might get it," Kevin said, rising from his chair. "You—saw—you noticed me, and you asked if I was okay, so I thought you might get it. And, actually, I think you do. You could make them do it differently next year. I know you won't be around at the time, you'll have graduated by then, but you could say something now. So all the next Year Ones don't have the same—shitty—time."

Andrew paused. He realised that he had decided, fairly early on in the interview, that Kevin would not really, at any point, make sense. But there was a logic to this suggestion. The yelling and crying was not without purpose: Andrew was being asked to be on its side. He had to refuse, of course, but he had to admit there was something to it.

"I could give the new councillors your feedback," he said at last. "After they're elected. They'll consider it. But it won't change the way they do things."

"They'll never listen at all if I say it. If you do, there's at least a chance."

"You have to be realistic. It's practically zero chance. And it won't change anything for you."

"A small chance is still a chance. It means something to me, already, that you listen."

Andrew shook his head. "You're completely crazy." It took him a moment to realise that he had said this out loud, and he flushed at his own indiscretion, but Kevin just gave him a small smile.

"I've heard that before," he said.

Andrew turned the conversation over in his mind all through the long bus ride home. While they had been talking, the subject of discussion had seemed intimately connected to Kevin's personal neuroses, indivisible from the odd figure barging his way into a forbidden space and weepily haranguing a stranger. But now, in the rumble of the upper deck, watching the orange-grey rows of streetlit flats parading past, Andrew could barely remember the boy's face. It was the matter itself that troubled him.

He thought, now, that Kevin was right about the bonding activities that were so popular in school. They favoured humiliation, domination, mastery over resistance. This was not an unfortunate side effect—it was designed into them. But there was no wisdom, he thought, in challenging this. Submission was required of you; and if you fought back, they just had to hurt you harder to get it. If you put too much of yourself out there, it was just that much more for them to cut down. You weren't safe unless they believed you'd given them what they wanted. You couldn't be a part of things unless you played the game. That was just how it was.

Kevin wasn't wrong to identify something grim in the lifetime of discipline that stretched before them. And the boy was right about his own role in it, too, Andrew thought, as his bus stop neared, and he clattered downstairs to stand, swaying, by the door. Kevin was a cautionary tale, an example of punishments to be avoided. Andrew felt sorry for him. But he couldn't afford more than pity. From a distance, pity. Andrew was going places, and he wasn't going to risk sharing that fate.

# DECEMBER 1999

THE CHALK BALL had grown thin, but Brian rubbed it anyway. He had a good set of calluses on his upper palms, the skin torn and reformed over months of training, but chalk always helped.

He took another moment to survey the elusive hold above him—an overgrown pimple of fake rock. Not that he expected new strategies to suggest themselves, after so many previous attempts. By now he was fairly certain of what he should do; it was just (just!) a question of execution. But he forced himself to go slowly. Desperate as he was to crack this route before they reordered the wall and it vanished, he'd learned that rushing would throw everything off, not just for a single climb but possibly the whole afternoon.

And now. The shimmy rightward, the tiny toe-tip hop, and he was on a single foot, the left, reaching carefully, carefully, with the other. Fingers splayed against the wall kept him in that sweet space between fallen forward and falling back. They didn't hurt yet, but they would later.

He was staring upward as his right foot found the nook. Barely a smudge in the wall. It was tempting to look down and fiddle with his position, but he knew from yesterday that this was as good as it got. There was nowhere safe to stand for long; you just had to keep going. So he rocked his weight straight over, stepping up into that perfect second when the strength in his thigh and calf and heel extended him with machine precision; when he knew where every gram of his body rested, and where every inch was headed. His hand swept up, gripped its target—his fingers fit, this time, easy as day—and then he scrambled up, the rest was trivial, done.

Later, as Brian climbed down, his muscles sounded with good clean empty pain. Like violin strings well bowed, filling the space around with a benign music. His faithful doubts came back only as he returned to ground. For many months they had formed themselves into questions—what else should he have done? What was he still missing, now?—which echoed uncomfortably through him. Brian had welcomed this. He should be uncomfortable, he'd thought.

More recently these questions had muted into quiet shadows, skirting the edge of his vision. Sometimes he went entire days without worrying about his own failures of memory; and instead of telling himself off, he replayed in his head Auntie Lay Choo's audacious kindness, her impossible line: "Brian, you didn't do a crime or what, don't need to punish yourself any more already." He could not acquit himself, but he could obey instructions: he would stop enforcing the loss of Andrew. It didn't need his enforcement; it was what it was.

As he left the hall he realised he'd ripped his hands again.

The familiar beeps came through the curtain as he soaped his body. He moved hastily to rinse and towel off, but the message that flickered onto the small pager screen didn't reward the effort:

*SICK, CANT COME SORRY. CALL ME NEXT WK? HAPPY NEW YEAR.*

He fought back disappointment. It might not have led anywhere, after all, and at least she'd said to call. Brian really liked her, though; and he knew this was all a bigger deal than it should be. Twenty-four and this was his first whisper of a date in seven years. He remembered the string of girlfriends in school, who had taken up an enormous amount of time and energy, until that whole business, when he was seventeen, at junior college, with Ting Ting.

The discovery that he liked Ting Ting arrived unexpectedly, after two months of pursuit and three of going steady. Mostly it made him realise that he hadn't much liked—or known—any of the other girls at all. He had liked the idea of them perched by him. He had liked making out. And, if he was honest with himself, he had liked most of all the small, unacknowledged movements from Darren and Ravi and the other guys at school, when they saw him with an arm around a cute girl. Their eyebrows flickering upward, their glances sharpening: infinitesimal salutes which affirmed that he was on safe ground. That he had achieved something with this one. He had liked all of that, but he hadn't really liked them, the girls.

Ting Ting ought to have done well by comparison, but instead he found himself wondering what he was doing with her. Or with any of them at all. The pleasure in holding her was muffled, as though it came through a thick barrier, and always with a distracting sense that something vital was missing. He didn't know what, though he pictured it, sometimes, peripherally, inconsequentially, as walls and platforms shifting. Layers and structures unfolding. Some more complete feeling just out of reach, as if he had forgotten a word for what he wanted to say.

Ting Ting adored him. He felt like a fraud.

"Are you crazy?" Darren's eyes were saucer-like. "Wahlau, you're never happy, man. Every five, six months got some new char bor. She's damn hot lorh." (Darren's appraisal, in fact, had prompted Brian to seek her out in the first place.) "And you yourself say you like her, and she's not like that super high maintenance one right?"

Brian shook his head. Here Darren meant Shuyi. The description was somewhat unfair. Shuyi hadn't demanded anything of Brian, exactly, but she'd had money in quantities alien to him, and thought nothing of going out to cinemas and bowling alleys and video arcades and fast food joints almost every day. She had always paid her own share, but even so, his pocket money simply hadn't been able to keep up.

"Yah, then?" Darren demanded. "If there's no problem, then what's the problem?"

He didn't really know. The problem was just that there was a problem.

"If you're not into her, then dump her," Hwee Leng said, sharply. Brian knew she meant well, but he did sometimes wish she would mince her words.

"But what if I'm just asking too much? There's nothing really *wrong*."

"I'm not spending hours talking about this, Brian. My advice is very simple. If you don't really, really want to be with her, then what's the point? It's mean to her to act like you care, if actually you don't. Dump her."

So he had. He felt a little bad about how awfully this tore her up, but a single dose of guilt was better than the sticky film of the stuff coating him constantly during his pantomime of affection. For the first time in years, there was a lapse in the stream of girls Brian brought home to while away afternoons in his bedroom: kissing, listening to tapes, doing a bit of homework together. Andrew, if he was home at all, sat wrapped in work at his desk, undisturbed. Brian and the girls rarely spoke; they were quiet as mice.

His mother noticed the end to the girlfriends and inquired.

"Don't have time now."

She made an approving noise in her throat. "Yah, good. A-Levels coming already. Better to concentrate on your studies first. Your mother and father didn't want to nag you when you started with that Cherilyn, we don't want to interfere in your these private things." (Unknown to Brian, this girl's appearance had in fact triggered a panicked parental conference, which cautiously resolved to wait-and-see: it was at least a girl, and a Chinese girl, this time.) "But A-Levels is an important year. Good that you are now matured enough to realised what the priorities are."

Nothing she said surprised Brian exactly, but at the time he found it odd that the matter was broached at all. As the boys reached their late teens, directives of this sort had slowed to a trickle and then dried into silence. No other mode of conversation grew up in its place. On many days, boys and parents said nothing to one another at all. The childhood ban on eating in front of the television was implicitly dissolved; more often than not Brian came home in the evening to find his parents on the sofas, plates on their laps, as casino showdowns and romantic rivalries played out fuzzily on the screen. Andrew's success, the luminescent promise of his future, had exceeded every reasonable demand. Kim Seng and Poh Ling could, perhaps, cut their sons a little slack. They seemed calmed then, reassured, safe.

Since then his dating life had been a simple blank. The drear military years hadn't helped, of course. But even in the bright new bubble of university he had held back. Sometimes Lay Choo ventured nervous queries, and dropped cryptic references to twins and genes and closets, giving him the vibe that—his early clarifications notwithstanding—she still thought he was maybe into boys, and frightened of it. He wasn't into boys at all, but only lately had he realised that the fear she sensed was a real thing. The threat of charged wires strung between himself and himself, an old distrust he was finally learning to test.

Brian didn't like extracting lessons from the photograph of Andrew. "What happened to him was his own thing. It shouldn't be like some kind of secondary school essay," he'd told Lay Choo during one of their coffee sessions. "Or a Chinese textbook chapter, there's always a moral of the story." He didn't want to be parasitic.

But he also couldn't help it. He looked at the picture with the selfishness of the survivor, and details kicked him. Hands on collarbone. Always, always, Andrew's face. He looked and he saw the forgotten fact of desire. This alone seemed to Brian a vast work of courage, one which shamed him. Andrew had wanted someone, despite its price. Brian could only recall, very thinly, that he had once known the shape of such a thing. Like ghosts through layers of tracing paper.

The picture tugged him the other way, too. Say he

reclaimed what he had lost—say he found a girl and it was really there this time, the startling movement beneath his feet. He was dogged by the feeling that he shouldn't take joy where his brother had found punishment. There shouldn't be any difference between them. If Andrew had been robbed, Brian had to steal from himself to balance the scales, or he would be an accessory to the original crime. He knew it was an absurdity, but it was taking him time to let it go.

Lay Choo was already at one of the tables outside the café when he arrived.

"Sorry, I just came from climbing, I had to shower first."

"Never mind, I came late also. Normally I never come this area, very far from Simei, and all the buildings so confusing."

"Sorry to make you come all the way."

"Never mind." She didn't begrudge her nephew the hour on three different buses, from her home in the east of the island to his campus in the west. Their meetings were too hard won for her to resent a little travel. "I get you a drink."

As she queued at the counter, Brian half-heartedly fought a cigarette, and lost. Next year, he told himself. Tomorrow. Or when this pack was through.

Sessions with his aunt no longer made him nervous. Sometime in the last ten months they had shed their novelty and their treacherous sheen. Or perhaps his treachery was now so commonplace, so complete, that it made no sense to fret about a few chats over tea, of all things. It helped that they'd given up trying to meet at his family flat, dodging and weaving about his parents' expected movements. He still wasn't always sure what to say to Lay Choo, but being with her felt ordinary now.

She returned with their cups. "So, how's it like living in the dorm?"

"Not bad. More convenient lah, don't have to travel all the way from Braddell to go for lectures. Also I can go to the university climbing wall a lot."

"Oh yah, you said just now. So this climbing is on a wall? Like that dangerous or not?"

"No lah, it's okay, the kind I do doesn't go very high."

"I never knew you did this climbing. Must be getting very strong."

"Last time in school I also did a bit, but not so much. Nowadays I have more practice, definitely getting better."

"Yah, very good, can just walk over whenever you feel like it." She paused. "And—how are your parents with you living out here?"

Brian shrugged. "They're not very happy, but you know what they're like, whatever I do they're also not very happy."

"Hmm." Lay Choo wasn't sure what to say to this. However impossible she found her brother, she could never fully shake the sense of wronging him at these moments. Sneaking around to meet his son was one thing; failing to reprove heretical remarks about parents was another. But she didn't have it in her to scold. She felt responsible for Brian, but she had no idea how to go about shaping another entire person. She met her nephew in order to talk and to listen, not to dispense moral education. Maybe it was just as well, she thought, that she would never have children.

"Here without them maybe you have a bit more privacy."

Brian tilted his head. It wasn't quite a nod. "How's Nurul?"

"She's okay," Lay Choo said. He'd started asking after Nurul recently, initially speaking of her only gingerly, and it was still a surprise and a pleasure. "She's quite worried, last few weeks her brother has been sick. Then she has to help her sister-in-law take care of the kids. But on Monday he came out of hospital already and doctor said should be okay."

"Hope he gets better soon."

"Thanks."

A breeze rattled round the open courtyard, sending a brown paper napkin swirling across the floor. Around them, students flashed one another white smiles and laughter, or pored over notes spilling from fat binders, neon highlighters at the ready. Just another afternoon cup of tea between friends, Brian thought, except that it wasn't. His brother was also at the table, as always; he was why they were together.

Brian needed this. With everyone else he had to act as though Andrew wasn't there, as if he had perhaps never existed. Just as bad, or worse, if he had to tell the story himself—"I used to have a twin"—to a whole new person, for whom Andrew had always been dead. He could see them working backwards from Brian as half a pair, undoubled. This was too convenient, unfair to Andrew, untrue. Thick crayon over the past's secretive filigree of silences. But Lay Choo had actually been with them, both of them: she knew as much as Brian did and would never pretend to know more.

There'd been Hwee Leng, too, of course, right after it all blew up, but the swollen phone bills had ended their cross-continental calls within a month. Email felt too final, too formal; and lately in Hwee Leng's messages her habitual outrage (which Brian could handle) was increasingly enmeshed among the springs and levers of busy political doings and academic theory (which he could not). He didn't want to crack codes; he just wanted company who would understand.

When Lay Choo's name first stole into his inbox back in February, a week after Chinese New Year and nearly a year after Andrew's death, Brian was wary. He couldn't imagine what she wanted with him. His parents must have put her up to it, he thought, except he couldn't see why they would do that, either. By then their interrogations and their threats had gone into frosty remission, replaced by a biting silence. Commissioning his aunt to perform fake friendliness seemed to Brian an unlikely change of tack.

He hadn't yet decided whether to reply when Lay Choo's follow-up arrived, tipping him over to yes. ("Btw pls dun tell ur parents I emailed u. I will explain to u why when we meet in person. Tks.")

Her story amazed him. The hidden histories, naturally—but also, especially, everything transacted right in front of him, only recently, when he was not a child or a fool any more (or so he'd believed). Even after everything, after Andrew, he hadn't noticed any of it: like Lay Choo's mere half an hour at Andrew's funeral, after Poh Ling had finally convinced her husband that complete absence would be an even greater disrespect than attending while lesbian. "And when I came, they were so cold, very cold." She could see that they wanted her to leave as soon as possible, so she had.

The end of the shared meals at Braddell, the phone calls flintily rebuffed, the strained dance of minimal civility at the New Year festivities: it had all passed Brian by. Throughout the reunion dinner gathering, Lay Choo observed Poh Ling watchfully steering her son away from his aunt. (It was unnecessary: wrapped in his own resentments, Brian hardly spoke to anyone.) Lay Choo sat by Ma's idling karaoke machine and stifled the urge to scream. If she didn't *do something*, she realised, they would play at this unconvincing game of happy families, from their placid private hells, forever.

"You had to work today?"

"Yah, supposed to be half day only, but because of this Y2K computer thing, my boss is very scared everything crash tomorrow, so then got all this last minute firefighting." Lay Choo sighed. "Never mind lah, at least can still leave work early. Are you going to celebrate?"

"Not really."

"What about your friends? I thought you young people, sure have a lot of parties."

"No lah," Brian said. "Actually I was going to meet someone, but she got sick."

"Oh, like that ah." Lay Choo thought it over. "Eh, we are cooking dinner, some of our colleagues coming to eat, you join also lah."

In place of the chimerical date, there would be a relative's flat, and a room full of middle-aged shoe shop staff. Brian would once have declined on autopilot. Some buried limbic centre still signalled to him: no. But he looked across the table now, at his brave, hopeful aunt, who had put out her hands from the merest toehold and hauled herself totally into his life, and he knew he was looking forward to it.

"Sure," he said. "Let's go."

# JUNE 1993

I N THOSE DAYS Sentosa lay between times. Its old Malay name of Pulau Blakang Mati, the Island of Death from Behind, was falling away forever, after two decades of tourist board investment, laying the bright hard infrastructure of a cable car line, cycle paths, a monorail system. The military fort built by the British, its virgin artillery retired, was now a staid museum. For some years it had housed a reluctant living exhibit, left-wing dissident Chia Thye Poh; but recently, almost thirty years after his initial arrest, and still without a charge to his name, he had been allowed to return to the mainland, leaving behind only wax figures and bored schoolkids. History had just about slipped away.

But there were still almost twenty years to go before the island's confident reinvention as a bubbly playground for the super-rich. Only much later would tinkling video advertisements on international flights hope to catch the Russian or the Chinese eye with rhapsodies about manicured waterfront apartments, free from capital gains or estate taxation. In 1993 no one had planned for the luxury casino or the Hollywood theme park that would offer safe moneyed substitutes for dreams. There was no hint of the coming wild-caught dolphins, with their fading ocean memories, made to turn tricks and grace corporate websites.

For now, Sentosa was a haphazard affair. The kitschy attractions that dotted its surface almost randomly had clearly been conceived in the cubicles of harried civil servants, desperate to bulk out the lists of bullet points in their draft memoranda on Leisure & Recreation. How else to explain the bumpy elevator ride, with flashing red lights, grandiosely dubbed Volcanoland? Or the mini golf course composed of eighteen largely identical rubberised oval patches? Despite this flaccidity, the island was popular enough, especially with teenagers. Its beaches were blandly pleasant, if small, and its well-paved paths saw a fair amount of use.

"Seriously, man, I get that she's sort of smart," Ming Wei was saying, as he dug his feet into the sand. "In that arty kind of way. Can talk very cheem, lots of highfalutin words, that type. But there are so many Ashford girls who are hot and smart lorh. So many smarter ones than her some more. She only got him because she is willing to be so—shameless and aggressive. Damn sad."

Brian leaned back against the tree and looked out across the sea. He was rather tired of this. Once Ming Wei set the little attack dogs of his attention into motion, they did not seem to rest until everyone else was bored into feigning agreement. The matter at hand was, as it had been for some weeks, the hideous breach in the rightful order of the universe caused by Andrew and Hwee Leng dating between castes. On the one hand, a brilliant, sporty, popular Ashford guy, destined for greatness; on the other, a thickset, loud-mouthed, acne-scarred weirdo from that pasture of mediocrity, Marine Parade Junior College. It was worse than an injustice: it was a violation of the natural laws of economics. It was market failure. Someone had to be punished for it; and so far, that person had mostly been Brian.

Initially Brian tried to deflect this sort of talk by reminding Ming Wei that he, personally, really rather liked Hwee Leng. She had, in fact, been Brian's friend long before she became Andrew's girlfriend. But this was in vain. Ming Wei wasn't talking about friends: you could be friends with any girl you wanted, if being friends with girls was your sort of thing; though Ming Wei himself always suspected most guys were just using the nebulous idea of "friendship" as flimsy cover to get closer to their targets, even if some of these guys tried to delude themselves otherwise, probably largely to save their own face when they were ultimately rejected—but anyway he digressed. He wasn't saying nobody could be friends with Hwee Leng; he'd even admit that she said the occasional amusing thing. But Brian was surely objective enough to see that when it came to relationships, his brother was—by every measure imaginable—way out of her league.

"And it's not just I say one, okay," he said. "Senior Minister also agrees with me."

"What?" The improbability of Singapore's pre-eminent elder statesman weighing in on his brother's teenage love life startled Brian out of indifference.

"Don't you know about this? It's always in the news. It's a threat to the survival of the country!" Ming Wei laughed. "Too many high quality men marrying low quality women these days. Graduate guys go for non-graduate women, graduate women don't get married. It's bad for the breeding pool. Only dumb women have kids, you don't get enough smart kids, and society goes downhill. So Andrew has a duty to Singapore to choose the right girlfriend! He's got valuable genes, cannot waste."

Brian waved a hand irritably. "Aiyah, what are you talking about—what marriage, kids, genes? People are in JC only, who is thinking about this kind of thing?"

"Joking only lah. But my point is this. You have to have standards—and even Lee Kuan Yew thinks so lorh. Your brother is so *zai*, he should look for the right girl."

Technically, *zai* denoted steadiness in the face of pressure, but as Ming Wei meant it, it was so much more. It was a statement of a guy's holistic worth, and it was the central organising principle of the social world. In addition to the basic unruffled air, you had to be good at school (but not a nerd), good at sport (but not a brainless jock), and good-looking (but not to care about it). (Ming Wei acknowledged only these criteria, though a standard array of class and racial prejudices hung behind them like so much suffocating wallpaper.) It was bad form to speak of *zai* other than as praise for a peer, because it was the antithesis of *zai* to admit to striving for it, or to worrying about how one stacked up; but Ming Wei had no doubt that secretly, or not so secretly, everyone did. They had to: it was everything. To be *zai* was to merit respect. And girls.

Girls were never, themselves, *zai*. A guy could demonstrate the refinement of his taste through a preference for girls who possessed good school pedigrees, and who were therefore certifiably smart and accomplished. But despite his facetious invocation of Lee Kuan Yew's eugenicist dreams, Ming Wei saw little value in female achievements in themselves. Girls certainly didn't get points for being yammering smart alecs of the Hwee Leng variety, especially when they looked like she did. If Andrew had picked up some polytechnic ah lian who was unable to string together a sentence in English, but who had big doe eyes or big tits, it would still have shaken his dignity, but it would at least have made some sense. Whereas consorting with the likes of Hwee Leng was a pure and senseless slap in the face. Andrew embodied the smart guy made good, the smart guy who was cool. Did he think so little of his own claims—and, by extension, those of all underserved smart guys everywhere—that he would settle for so little? Ming Wei took it personally.

No one properly shared Ming Wei's outrage. At school his tirades were received with distant sympathy, and with amusement that Andrew, so famously aloof with girls, had finally succumbed, and to such a creature, too. But, without seeing her themselves, the others had to reserve judgment. The grating intensity of Hwee Leng's personality was difficult to convey secondhand; and if Ming Wei could not supply a smoking gun, such as obesity or disability, it was always possible that she was not quite as ugly as he claimed. No, the only person in any position to fully appreciate the problem was Brian, and he was gallingly insensible of the horror he had helped to bring about.

Brian had met Hwee Leng about a year and a half earlier, when they were sixteen going on seventeen, both newly arrived at Marine Parade Junior College. He belayed her on a climb at an early Outdoor Club meeting, they got to talking, and they became friends. It was simple. Left to himself he would never have noticed anything unusual: he met her before he met the general view of her about school. She never struck him as "scary, like quite bossy like that" (Darren) or "trying way too hard to make up for being an ugly chick" (Ravi). He didn't transmit these opinions to her, but she knew about them anyway.

"People like Ravi don't like me," she told him once, "because I know where I am in their stupid little Venn diagrams and league tables of the world, but I won't just roll over and accept it. I don't pretend their garbage makes any sense. You're a relief, Brian, you don't make all this continual fucking *commentary*, like we're all horses running in the Turf Club."

Brian did not usually introduce his friends to his brother, but Hwee Leng had asked to speak to Andrew to get advice on universities abroad. Every year, Ashford graduates spilled out into colleges across the globe on the lion's share of Singapore government scholarships, with many more wealthy enough to self-fund their way. Rumour had it that Ashford sent more kids to Harvard than did any other school in the world. In this hothouse of anticipation, a thicket of support had sprung up: alumni were at hand to answer questions about every institution, and a separate teacher advisor assisted with each destination country. The corridors filled with the sound of British and American admissions jargon: "SATs", "UCAS", "Early Admission", "need-blind aid". Marine Parade's smaller band of hopefuls, like Hwee Leng, did not have access to such resources.

They first met one Saturday evening at McDonald's. (Hwee Leng would later wince at this detail, but it made perfect sense: it was air-conditioned, and they could stay as long as they liked without being chased away.) Andrew, fresh from a badminton victory, had his doubles partner and classmate Ming Wei in tow.

"You going for a government scholarship?" Ming Wei managed to ask, between mouthfuls of burger, within fifteen seconds of Hwee Leng sitting down. He was a tall boy with a lean build, an expressive mouth, and large hands which he tended to wave generously as he spoke.

"No, I don't think so."

"One of those ah! Father-mother scholarship. Lucky, lucky. What course are you going to do?"

"I'm not totally sure yet, but probably sociology."

"What! *Sociology*?" The word lengthened, in his mouth, into something unreal. "What are you going to do with that afterwards? *Teach*?" His voice peaked in disbelief. "And your parents are paying some more? Wah, don't you think it's a waste of their money to do something without a good career path? Like that might as well go to a local uni. Are you in the arts stream now?" (The arts stream, in the Ashford cosmology, was a dustbin for also-rans, who couldn't handle the genuine intellectual rigour of the sciences.)

"Yes, actually. Do you need to know all my teachers' names also? My address and IC number? I had kaya on toast for breakfast this morning—quick, you should be writing this down."

Ming Wei drew back in mock fear. "Relax, woman, people are just curious only, what's the big deal."

Things between those two had remained on more or less the same footing in the two months since then, even as—to Brian's surprise—Hwee Leng began calling their home and asking to speak to his brother; and Andrew started to spend long late hours in the small corridor where the phone sat; and they both suggested hanging out as a group. For Brian, who lacked Ming Wei's detailed sexual ideology, the main strangeness of it lay in suddenly seeing so much of his brother socially: something he hadn't done, as far as he could recall, since they had been eleven or twelve, before Andrew had been inducted into his bright new world.

The subjects of Ming Wei's lecture, as he browbeat Brian on the Sentosa beach, were shuffling side by side along a footpath, which formed a small ellipsoidal loop a little to the northwest. It was a fresh, breezy day—unusually good weather for June—and Hwee Leng, her spirits high, was inevitably talking.

"You want to feel sorry for him," she said. "It's not fair that people are so mean about all these things that aren't important, like him being short, and his hair and his ugly bag and all that." (Here she meant Chinh, a notorious figure of fun in her school, who had once been tied to the goalpost at one end of the basketball court. He might have stayed there all night if a cleaner hadn't happened to spot him.) "But he really makes you not want to care. My classmate

Michelle is one of the few people who is nice to him, and yesterday he said to her, just out of the blue, Michelle, you're shallower than a fat girl should be." (Michelle had burst into tears.) "After that kind of thing, I just can't feel any more sympathy. I mean, yah, just because he's a jerk doesn't mean other people should be jerks to him, but—he doesn't do himself any favours."

"That's hard," Andrew said. "When there are both good and bad reasons why he doesn't have friends."

"Exactly. The bad reasons stay bad reasons, even if there are also good ones. And the other way around."

Hwee Leng risked a quick glance, searching Andrew's face. A month on and she still didn't know how to reckon it, her good luck with this boy, its delights suspended in a tense, crackling field—like static—which she felt herself always crossing. She felt safest talking: she knew he thought her clever (and she agreed); she sensed he approved (which she approved in turn). That meant a lot, after a lifetime—or so seventeen seemed—of being told, by just about everyone around her, that she made everything way too "complicating". He listened; and this was such a rare token of regard, so simple and so great.

But she couldn't shake the apprehensive sense that she wanted too much. The world lit up when he was near, and he was often near; what more could she ask? It was ungrateful to feel so wretchedly deprived by the half-metre (that was the current gap) between their hands. She could and did lob every finely worded opinion fearlessly across, but she couldn't discharge this tingling weakness in her fingers. When they were together, the thought of his skin seized her constantly, sometimes with an urgency that felt like pain. She'd made a move a few precious, unsatisfactory times—a hand on his knee, her head on his shoulder, timid hugs as they'd parted—and Andrew hadn't discouraged her exactly, he hadn't demurred or moved away, but he never returned her gestures either.

She didn't know what to make of this. Her sexual experience to date consisted largely of periods of blank agony, in which she brushed her lips against the back of her hands, and dreamt formless dreams of skin and bone; and also of irregular incidents, which she didn't like to think about, of unsuccessful, solitary probing in the dark, breath anxiously withheld, her hands pulling back quickly at any sharpness of sensation. The dynamics of mutual desire were a mystery. She formed uncharacteristically flat theories: Andrew was too polite, perhaps; perhaps he had higher things on his mind. She had never been thought pretty, and it made a certain kind of sense, to her, that he might be happy to enter into an intimacy, to accept her bright, crystalline conversational offerings, without finding her physically compelling. This might be the best she could reasonably hope for. She was in his space on sufferance, on grace; she had no right to be wanted. She should not complain.

(She would never have offered Brian such dreadful advice.)

Andrew smiled at her now, but only for a second: as she returned it his gaze was already flickering off and away.

"Why don't we go sit over there?"

He indicated a large square picnic table, framed by thick, backless benches on each side. As they approached, Hwee Leng hovered strategically at one corner, wondering how she should best position herself to make any physical contact seem natural. But Andrew slid himself into the middle of the far side, so that the most she could do, without embarrassment, was shuffle along the adjoining edge, until they were sitting in a sort of L shape.

"Something kind of weird happened to me the other day," Andrew said, tracing a clover pattern on the table with his fingernail.

"Oh? What?"

"It was about a week before term ended."

"You didn't mention anything before." They'd spoken at least five or six times since.

"It's a bit of a funny story," he said. "I've been—quite disturbed by it. Thinking about it quite a lot."

She waited. She had no concept, she realised, of what might disturb him. After a few more moments' scratching, he spoke.

"There's this Year One, I don't really know him, but he came to me at the start of the year. He had some kind of problem with Orientation Week, he didn't like the activities. I think he just wanted to talk about it to someone on the Council. Anyway, after that he went away." He looked up at her briefly, then returned his attention to the imaginary clover. "Then the other day Mr de Souza—the Head of Discipline—asked this guy to help me pack the flags away after assembly, and when we were in the store room, he brought this thing up again."

"What thing?"

"He had this problem with Orientation, he didn't like it, he felt like people were forcing him to do tau pok and stuff like that. Anyway, it was going to be his birthday soon, and he said some guys in his class were going to bring some deep heat, you know, that cream stuff for when your muscles hurt after sport. When you put it on, it makes your skin feel like it's burning. And—" He coloured here. "—he said they said they were going to put it on his dick."

"That's horrendous!"

"Yeah, he wasn't very happy about it."

"Of course not! That's terrible! Did he go to a teacher?"

"I don't think so. I mean, it's kind of normal, you know. As in," he went on quickly, seeing her face, "I think they'd already done it to a lot of other guys in his class, so it's not like—it's supposed to be just for fun."

Hwee Leng shook her head angrily. "I don't believe that for a moment. Maybe some stupid guys with some stupid idea of being macho think it's fun, but if he doesn't want it, then it's just—screwed up."

"That's the sort of thing he said."

He smiled at her as he said this, and—rather shamefully—she allowed herself to be disarmed. But she persisted a little. "Someone has to stop this—or at least not let them just get away with it. Someone should say something. If he won't tell a teacher, you have to do it."

"No one else is complaining; and if he gets them into trouble, things will be worse for him. Anyway, he kept saying I mustn't tell anyone about it."

This was the final word for Hwee Leng. From the age of eight she had suffered in bitter impotence the parents who openly read her diary, who rummaged through notes and letters from her friends, and who laughed at her protests, at first tearful and now stony. "Aiyoh, so drama mama until like that! What *privacy*? Please! What is so bad in here that you want to hide from your father and mother? You were come out of your mother's stomach one, you know!" Something abject in her gut cried out at this—I didn't *ask* to owe you!—but it was true, she lived in their home, and ate the rice they put on the table, and so she must give way. In a lifetime full of such rotten compromises, keeping a confidence was one of the few good deeds wholly in her power; and so, if this boy desired secrecy, then secrecy must be counselled.

"The poor guy," she said to the table.

"Yeah," Andrew sighed. He seemed suddenly very grave. "I don't know why he told me about it. I don't really know him also. We're not like—I only ever talked to him once or twice before. Do you think it's a bit weird for him to tell me?"

"Not at all. It probably makes him feel better to tell someone."

"But why me? It doesn't have anything to do with me."

"Maybe he just thought you would be a good person to talk to, after that first time."

"You don't think there's something funny going on? Like, he's telling me for some funny reason? Like he has some kind of strange ideas about me or anything? I've felt kind of—weird—about it."

"No lah, why would there be a problem? People need to talk about things. It's just natural. Maybe you just come across like someone he can trust." She paused, nerving herself. "I mean—I'd trust you."

She was rewarded with another smile, broader this time, warmer, more open; and then, natural as daylight, he reached across the table and enclosed her right hand in his.

"I'm really glad I could tell you about this," he said.

Astonished by her triumph, she looked away.

When the twins got home, Andrew entered their bedroom with relief, a relief that felt like great happiness. It was too late to start work on them tonight, but he looked with anticipation at the neat leaves of paper on his desk, the stack of fat, friendly books with their clear curves and sparse, pregnant notations. Tomorrow he would make his way through the material he had put off for the last two weeks.

There had been too much of the other lately—evenings with the pages open in front of him but unread, unreadable, as he mulled over the shifting, jumbled fragments of... of what? Of nothing, really. Nothing had happened, and it had, in any case, nothing to do with him.

He was able to return to this diagnosis now that he'd spoken to Hwee Leng, putting the event, such as it was, in proper perspective. He'd known from the first that it did not merit his attention, but aimless details had persisted: the fierce morning sun outside; the pattern of shuttered shadows on the dark wood of the hall floor; the weave of the flags, rough and dusty against his fingertips. A small gold cross twinkling in the brown of Kevin's neck. "Leila transferred in March," the other boy had said despondently. "She went to Republic JC. I wanted to change too, but my parents said it's better to stay in Ashford. Top JC and all that. Nobody here gets it, Andrew—you're the only person who even listened to me." As he said this he laid light fingers in the crook of Andrew's arm. Under the weight of his pleading, round-eyed stare, Andrew thought of the small polished wood metronome in the music room. He felt like he was on the end of that curious inverted pendulum, tipping forward with agonising slowness, and then righting himself again.

But this was all nothing, and it had nothing to do with him. Even the sudden electric race of his heartbeat, and the distinct stiffness in his crotch, which he identified with clear-eyed detachment. Andrew was pragmatic about the body. He acknowledged the fundamental randomness of its machine parts. As its uncountable molecules clicked together in their unfathomably complex game of three-dimensional billiards, messy things were bound to spill over now and then; you couldn't avoid the occasional meaningless spikes of chemical noise. In his view, there was nothing so magical about an erection. If you could wake up from a dreamless night with a hard-on—if the organ could stir as you dried the dishes, or as you revised for a history test on the Anglo-Dutch Treaty of 1824—it only stood to reason that you could have a corporeal sexual response to any human contact, even with boys. With Andrew's many years in all-male schools, his primary human contact had in fact been with boys. This had happened before, and passed without consequence: there was no reason to attribute significance to it now.

Yet it nagged at him. Not Kevin's problem, this time, but the boy himself, his high-wire urgency, the restless animation of his hands, the hopeful curve of his lower lip. Quite by accident, Andrew noticed, two days later, that he was walking behind Kevin, between tutorials, and something in him tightened at the sharp line of hair at the nape of the other boy's neck, and the neatness of his narrow hips. He almost went past his class but stopped himself just in time. He sat and stared numbly at the teacher for the next forty minutes.

It occurred to him that he must have seen Kevin around school scores of times before, and paid no mind. After their first meeting, in January, he would have had difficulty picking the other boy out of a line of seventeen-year-olds of similar height and colour, though the triangle of his build and the long fall of his fringe seemed now so very individual. The last day of term came and went without any further encounter; and Andrew felt an odd disappointment settle over him as he made the last lone humid trek to the bus stop, for the journey home, and the four weeks away. The erection visited again that night, revenging itself on him, as he lay in a wakeful grey stasis, resentful of the logistical difficulties presented by sharing a bed with his brother. (Resentful—and also grateful. Because he wasn't really going to jerk himself off to thoughts of this guy, was he? There was being pragmatic about things, and then there was—who knew what that was.)

It was absurd. He had a girlfriend. It was nothing. He had a girlfriend. The late night phone calls with Hwee Leng continued, and through them all Andrew remained impeccably attentive. It took great conscientiousness, but he managed. He was exhausted, each night, as the phone clicked back into its plastic cradle—exhausted enough to think, with some hope, as he rubbed his eyes in the bathroom fluorescence, of untroubled slumber. But desire rose again to torment him once he was back in the dark of his bed. Brian slept through it all.

Before this began, talking to Hwee Leng had been the only thing—other than mathematics—which carried the tang of those crisp few Moscow days. Hwee Leng came at things from unusual angles; she strayed from well-trodden circles of speech. He had to work at their conversation, and the work had until recently been rewarded with all the real pleasure of genuine interest. "I ask everyone why they like what they like," she had said when they first met. "I love it when people really like things. I can't stand it when they say they are sian, not just like when they are forced to sit in a boring assembly or something like that, but when they are—permanently—sian, like it's become a part of who they are." He recognised this description. The possibility of this fate had disturbed him ever since his time in Russia.

Like him, Hwee Leng was impatient to escape the purgatorial confinement of these last long school days. So much of their talk was of a dazzling future in an unknown land, shimmering on the road just ahead of them, almost within reach. "What gets me is, it has to be even more different than we can imagine," she said. "There'll be all this—new—stuff. What I'm really looking forward to is all the things I don't even have a picture of to look forward to yet, the fact that they're there, if that makes any sense." It did to Andrew; and when they spoke, he nearly had the feeling of building it.

But this comforting sense was dashed, now; lost, for Andrew, in an uncharacteristic lather of guilt and distraction. He needed it back. But what could he do? The ragged ends of loose impulses batted about in the aimless winds of his unease. He began with the thought that there was no need to tell Hwee Leng about Kevin, because it was nothing. This idea was thin enough to start, but as he clung to it through too many waking nights, it grew threadbare, and gave way, rottingly, to fear. Fear that he simply could not tell her, because honesty was impossible: had been made impossible, by some deep malformation in his nature from which this all sprang. And then, seamlessly logical, came the conviction: he must talk to her about it, he must, precisely because the talk itself would prove that this was all nothing, and there was nothing wrong.

He would come clean. He was not an especially verbal boy, but the words stuck with him now: he would come clean.

And so, today, he had. It felt good, he thought, a little light-headedly, to have told her everything.

Andrew had once read that a Rubik's Cube could be twisted into forty-three quintillion positions. This number was unimaginable, twenty digits long. Only fifty-four flat squares of colour, and the ways to arrange them outnumbered all the people who had ever been on the planet. But that was just from turning the Cube's faces. A few years ago, his friend Eng Siang had sabotaged Andrew's Cube: he'd ripped pieces out and stuck them back in differently, producing a configuration that Andrew hadn't been able to solve, no matter how hard he tried. He'd looked the problem up in the school library, and it turned out you could make twelve times as many combinations that way, but more than ninety percent of them would leave you frustrated forever, if you played by the rules. It felt like cheating, but you had to pull the rogue pieces out of the structure entirely, and put them back in manually, one by one, to restore the possibility of order.

Tonight Andrew felt like someone had done this with his mood, wrenched displaced elements back into legal grooves. Things weren't all in the right places yet, but the game was no longer rigged against him. It was only, once more, a matter of logical effort, and of time.

Samuel de Souza, chemistry teacher and Head of Discipline at Ashford Junior College for some seven years now, enjoyed sauntering through the white, airy spaces of the school, pausing in strategic places—the canteen with its long benches, the perimeters of the sports fields, the high-ceilinged front foyer—to remind the young men and women in his care that authority was present. He habitually stood with his hands behind him, one folded loosely over the other. A small man, with a barrel-like torso, he kept a very straight back. He was fond of reminding his students about the importance of posture, and of rearranging them as they sat, prodding their spines and pulling their shoulders back.

De Souza took his job seriously. He knew, he had been told often enough, sometimes with an air he didn't like, that discipline was a different job altogether at the neighbourhood schools. Yusof, at their last meet-up, had spoken of teens huddled in stairwells over bags of glue, and of blows exchanged by snarling boys, with older brothers covered in the curling blues and greens of gangland tattoos. Much worse than anything de Souza dealt with, of course; but, in de Souza's opinion, the very intractability of these problems lessened, in a sense, the value of his old classmate's role. Suppose you worked hard—as he was sure Yusof did— and eked out some semblance of order. Say you pulled the students more or less in line, and communicated enough rudimentary understanding of the syllabus so that it wasn't completely futile for them to sit the examinations. At the end of all that, you were still hampered by the quality of the raw materials you were given. You still produced only bus drivers, shop assistants, at best small businesspeople or minor clerks. Society's drones. It was running to stand still.

But at Ashford—at Ashford you shaped the nation. Future ministers, embryonic lawyers, inchoate doctors and professors: they passed through these rooms in their wet clay forms; they sat looking up at you from their tidy rows of chairs, their quick minds hungrily taking in every influence. And it was here that de Souza came in. Cleverness alone would not instil in these future leaders of Singapore the necessary sense of community or of pride. For that you needed order; order that went beyond the mere absence of the most overt disruptions, like smoking, shouting or public displays of affection. It took finer rules, with subtler purposes, to maintain the delicate calibrations of atmosphere so crucial to the students' moral development. To this end, de Souza carried, at all times, a clear plastic ruler, with which he measured suspect watch faces. Those with a diameter exceeding three and a half centimetres were confiscated. (A small collection of timepieces lived, as a result, in the bottom drawer of de Souza's desk.) He scanned the seas of shoes as students passed, and issued warnings if he detected anything but the plainest, most sober white. Three warnings in a term earned an afternoon's detention, from which fidgeting, chatter, books and magazines were forbidden—it was a time for silent homework, or else silent reflection.

He made no apologies for this meticulous attention to detail. It might seem harmless for a small loop of shirt to hang out over a waistband, for a boy's hair to curl down almost to his shoulders, or for a girl's skirt to creep a fraction of an inch above her knees; but it only took a few such deviations, fewer than you might imagine, for the careful harmony of the whole to be ruined. If there was one lesson he feared these bright Ashford sparks might not learn, it was how to subordinate themselves to the greater plan. To recognise that even as they sat at the top—perhaps especially as they sat at the top—they must think of themselves first and foremost not as individuals, but as parts of a bigger picture. Keeping the student body looking perfect was just an expression of, and training in, this deeper ethos.

It was de Souza's considered opinion—which he patiently shared, without admonition, with any student who asked—that the more seemingly pointless the regulation, and the more apparently unfairly enforced, the better. The truth was, life would never be reasonable. Poverty once made this clear to young people from an early age; but in these times of unearned plenty, it was easier for the immature to hang on to fantastical and self-indulgent ideas. It fell to de Souza, as a member of the older generation, to help them to recognise reality—to get over their self-importance, and accept their roles in society.

He was generally less concerned about the boys. National Service would teach the boys what they needed to know soon enough. Polishing and re-polishing boots into the dead of the night, under the threat of a gruelling round of push-ups if an officer found the tiniest speck: though often the boots were spotless, and the push-ups had to be done anyway. Talk back and you might find yourself in the detention barracks, where disgraced soldiers, stripped to their underwear, moved pyramids of sandbags—bag by back-breaking bag—from one end of a room to the other, before collapsing to sleep on coarse straw sacks. Experiences like these had shaped de Souza's philosophy, and he flattered himself that his boys emerged from school more prepared for recruit life than most.

But the girls were another matter. Good, simple girls were an endangered breed these days. Every year more of them struck him as spoilt, and there was no promise of National Service to beat it out of them. In these modern times you couldn't be sure that marriage would sort them out, either—many thought themselves "liberated" and might not marry at all, and those who did might still cow their poor husbands into who knows what kind of arrangement. Most of the girls in his school couldn't even cook! And there was a worrying tendency, among a growing few, to show a form of hideously fashionable conceit—to think the world owed them respect, even if they had no idea of how to behave themselves properly.

The case of one such girl was vexing him at the moment. Her name was Leila Ismail and she wasn't even at Ashford any more; she had transferred out, three months before, with the other Year Ones whose provisional acceptances had been withdrawn when their final O-Level exam results proved inadequate. In de Souza's opinion, having looked her over as she sat in his office—her hair in a frizzy, leonine cloud which she kept tugging with one hand, her fingernails heavily chewed—this was just as well. Academic weakness aside, there was an air of chaos about her which didn't fit with his view of the Ashford student. She moved too much, and her face worked into a series of arrogant responses as he spoke—fine, pencilled eyebrows drawing together, lips curling in doubt. She even interrupted him, more than once.

He had this sense even before hearing the wild complaint she had brought, beginning (as was the way with such people) with the most dramatic overstatement she could find. "One of the boys here raped me." She said this breathlessly, almost triumphantly, it seemed to him; and went on to give a name and class, from which de Souza recalled a clever, mild-mannered presence in one of his Year Two chemistry groups. A more gullible teacher, faced with such a sensational allegation, might have panicked and launched a witch hunt. But de Souza kept his calm. He didn't want shocking accusations; he wanted facts.

And duly got them, with a few simple inquiries. It turned out that this—incident—had taken place in February. Why had she waited so long to step up with her story? A full four months. "It's more like three—" she butted in, but he shut her up with a wave of his hand. According to her, it had happened in school; yet she couldn't identify anyone who might have been around. Whyever not? There were often students around on a Friday night, weren't there? It seemed they had been in the second floor male toilet; which naturally prompted the question, what was she doing there? The answer was, apparently, that he'd asked her to go in with him.

Didn't this strike her as a rather strange thing to do? Did

she make a habit of going into the male toilet? She was silent, here, and the incessant picking at her hair increased in pace. What—de Souza continued forensically—what precisely was the nature of her relationship with this boy?

"He was my boyfriend," she said, after a long pause. "But it doesn't matter! I didn't—I didn't want it."

But she'd been in the toilets with him before?

She said nothing.

What had they done there, before?

Still she said nothing.

De Souza sighed heavily. "Listen," he said. "I cannot do anything if I don't have the facts. You come to me with this story, you cannot expect that I don't ask you any questions, correct? Someone ask me to discipline a student, okay!" He brought a palm down, sharply, on his desk. "Just like that, I do it. No questions asked, I just punish this boy. Cannot be, right?"

Leila considered this for a while, her eyes on the poster on the wall behind him. Against a hospital-green background it depicted an oversized and smiling cartoon heart—an anatomical heart, not a symbol—wearing jogging shoes. It was accompanied by two impossibly large-eyed, white-toothed and glossy-haired cartoon students. De Souza, impatient, was about to try again, when she spoke, rapidly:

"Okay. Yes. We sometimes went in there, to—to have some privacy." She coloured. "But that day, I *didn't want it*. I told him only—only with a condom." De Souza kept his face scrupulously blank as she turned her tense gaze to his. "And he wanted—not to—he wanted to do it without one—so I didn't want to, but—he still did it."

She took a deep breath, and released it noisily. There. She'd said it. Again. That must be enough, now.

De Souza got up abruptly and turned to face his bookshelf to hide his annoyance. He hadn't invited this conversation to begin with, and now it had suddenly become even more distasteful than before. To think that all this disgusting behaviour had been going on—right here, beneath his very nose—and for her to bring such things up so shamelessly—it sickened him. But he couldn't afford to get emotional. He had a job to do. He turned back.

"Why didn't you report this right away?"

Something, an edge in his voice, alarmed Leila. She looked up at the soft-faced man standing ramrod straight in front of her, and the wave of urgent confidence that had carried her to the office that day began to ebb away. Stay focused, she told herself; answer what you have to, and we'll get there. He mustn't get away with this.

"It was—very difficult," she said. "Very—emotionally—mentally—difficult." Impossible to speak of the questions she had put to Ben, again and again, as if they were relevant: did you love me? Do you care? It is all okay with us? For weeks she had wanted nothing more than a sign that she mattered to him: because then, applying the backward logic of human decency, he could never have done what he had done. His bona fides, once established, would scrub the past clean of the act. After an age of tussling, Ben became imperious, bored; he began to put the phone down on her; and only then did she see the falseness of her premises. It didn't matter what she got him to say, or not say: those minutes when he had split her open were an unarguable wound. "I needed—I needed some time to think."

"A very long time," de Souza observed.

Again the note of challenge. This didn't seem to be going in the right direction. "What are you going to do?" she asked, trying to fight down panic.

"What am I going to do? I told you already what I am going to do. First I must find out what actually happened—"

"I told you what happened. I told him I didn't want it, and he did it. You can ask him. Ask him!"

"Don't tell me how to do my job." De Souza was coming to dislike this girl more with every minute. Barging into his office with such melodramatic, attention-seeking stories would have been aggravating enough, even if she were still at Ashford, and even if they had been true. What more when they turned out to be liberally embellished accounts of her own irresponsible behaviour. The girl had as good as admitted her own willing participation in this scandal: she objected only that it hadn't gone in the exact way she had wanted. De Souza wasn't employed by Singapore's premier junior college to settle silly squabbles between wayward youths about precisely how they degraded themselves. And what with the fishy timing, who knew if even this was the real complaint, or just a lurid invention to exact petty revenge for some imagined slight by an ex-boyfriend.

The lens of this thought brought his view into razor-sharp focus. The whole business must be something of that kind. A genuine victim would obviously have gone to the police straight away. Having decided this, he was loath to probe any further. There was no telling how much more sordid the tale would become, what manner of fetid detail would be unearthed, if he continued to stir the muck. Leila was visibly agitated, now, her shoulders hunched tightly, her teeth slightly bared. He just wanted her to go away.

"Don't tell me how to do my job," he repeated, and cleared his throat. "You have given me your side of the story; I will consider the case and the school rules, and take appropriate action."

She watched, confused, as he began to purposefully tidy the small stack of papers on his table.

"But is that all?"

"What do you mean is that all?"

"I mean—are you going to talk to him? What's going to happen?"

"I told you," he said, with deliberate patience. "I will

consider the case, and the school rules, and take appropriate action. I cannot rush into doing anything now. Unless," he added, as they stared at each other, "there is anything else you want to tell me about your—prior activities—with this boy."

It was a trap, she knew. There was nothing she wanted less to talk about. It was this thread, yanked from her, which had thrown the whole meeting into a snarl; but now it was offered as the only way to buy a continued audience. His mode of questioning had been distressing, but she was frightened of what it meant that it had stopped. What could lie behind this total phase shift, from pushing for so many uncomfortably private details, to seeming to want to know nothing at all? The vicious certainty unfurled in her, like a black flag, that he was just trying to get rid of her. And that he would succeed. She knew, she had known, she should never have come here at all.

And that had been de Souza's morning: an unwelcome but mercifully brief excursion into the seamy side of the world of youth. He knew there were certain merits to "exposure", as he called it. It was good for you, in the way everything unpleasant was, to skim the knowledge of how messed up other people could be. But still he was glad that the class of people he dealt with at Ashford made such experiences rare. The biggest nightmare of his career to date had been that hopeless girl, Ming-jun or Ting-jun or something like that, who had tried to kill herself because she had been pregnant. It had created weeks—weeks!—of fuss and anxiety for de Souza and the rest of the Ashford administration. He'd never wanted so badly to slap someone and tell her to get a grip.

He had hopes that this latest affair would prove—or had already proven—far simpler. But even so, even after her departure, Leila left toxic eddies of disruption in the air, and, finding it hard to concentrate, de Souza took the short walk to Commonwealth Hawker Centre to have an early lunch of roast duck rice and ice kachang.

He regretted the ice kachang now, back in his office. Too much for the middle of the day. The beans and the rich dark meat sat uneasily together in his guts. He tried not to belch.

He was meant to be planning a new staff training programme, but his mind returned, reluctantly, to one final aspect of the morning's sorry saga. That was the matter of the boy, Benjamin Chia of 2S01B. Not a superstar, but still a consistent performer, and widely thought a good candidate for next year's civil service scholarships. He spoke of an engineering degree somewhere in the States. His friends were all cut from the same polite, hard-working mould. None had ever come before de Souza with his Head of Discipline hat on.

De Souza had no intention of burdening Benjamin Chia with the girl's more overwrought charges, the r-word and such. There remained, however, the question of the boy's possible inappropriate behaviour on school premises. Getting up to that sort of thing in the toilets was serious misconduct, for which, ordinarily, de Souza would not hesitate to issue a strong reprimand; even to call the boy's parents. But in this case, de Souza felt strangely unwilling to act.

It was the human factor, he thought, the unfortunate human factor. On paper, and according to the purest principles, there were infractions on each side. On Benjamin's part an error of judgment, a lapse in decorum. But de Souza was sure, having encountered both parties, that the fundamental wrongness, the real moral fault, lay with the girl. A girl who could say "not without a condom" to his face. A girl who blithely advertised her own shamelessness, and who could even go as far as to fashion, from it, a sense of grievance. If a girl had grown so wild, then—if one examined the problem honestly—what boy, at that age, could not be led astray? (De Souza remembered being a boy of that age.) And pragmatically speaking, it appeared the danger was now past; the agent of disruption had been excised from the Ashford environment. There should be no future cause for worry.

De Souza was not making excuses for Benjamin Chia. Not at all. But it would be misguided, in the discharge of his role, to have no regard for proportion. If he took action, and especially if parents were involved, there could be a paper trail. This didn't just have potential consequences for the boy's future (otherwise so promising!) It might also have the disturbing side effect of lending credence to Leila Ismail and her complaints. As an outcome that was surely wrong. Anything which detracted from a full rejection of the values behind her outrageous claims must be avoided.

As this all clicked into place for de Souza, he began to wonder at his own easy credulity in letting things get so far. From everything he had seen and heard, it was just as probable that the entire story was a pack of lies from top to bottom. There was no reason to suppose that Benjamin Chia had ever laid a hand on the girl at all. Imagine the embarrassment if de Souza had raised the matter and shown himself to be taken in! Clarity flooded in and he almost laughed with relief. That was enough time-wasting. There was proper work to do.

The large and steeply sloping hall was thinly populated. From Ming Wei's seat, about a third of the way up, the team from Marine Parade looked awkward and boxy in their ill-fitting burgundy blazers. A nervous, angular, moonfaced girl; a runty nerd with a fiercely receding hairline and a permanent glare; and that Indian friend of Hwee Leng's. Ming Wei was unimpressed, and would have said so, but with Hwee Leng sitting on Andrew's other side, you couldn't count on him not to be in that irritating, moony, brainwashed state, where instead of laughing at jokes that Ming Wei *knew* he knew were funny, he would murmur something inane about "everyone having different taste" or some comments "not being very nice". It was extraordinary—and disgusting—the effect Hwee Leng had.

But at least Andrew had the excuse, however poor, of an unreasonable girlfriend. His brother, on the other hand, was just dull. Ringingly dull, all the way down. (It really made you pause and rethink this whole genetics thing, didn't it?) Watch his face when you spoke and you couldn't see the cogs turning in there; all you got was puzzled, bovine silence. So there was no point trying for intelligent understanding from that quarter, either. They would have to just watch this bunch of clowns in bored, frustrated silence.

Familiar sensations, Ming Wei reflected. These days, around Andrew, he was all too frequently unimpressed, bored, press-ganged into holding his tongue. It wasn't as if he minded being quiet when it was appropriate. You didn't go to his sort of school without learning soon enough to discipline your voice. Sometimes you had to still it—for the duration of the weekly assembly lectures, say, on the Ashfordian spirit or Singapore's unique multi-racial society or putting community before self. And sometime you had to lend it to the wider group, as he had every morning for twelve years, chanting the national pledge and singing the national anthem. The point was, he knew when to take things seriously, and when to relax. Whereas Hwee Leng was the wrong way round: chafing and fussing against all kinds of normal, but bizarrely reverent toward the laughable. You couldn't joke around her. She'd almost turned green when Ming Wei was telling Andrew what Benjamin had told him about the dance club slut's latest drunken exploits. "One of those horse face ones, but you know, body's not bad, can always cover the face, bang the base. But wahlau eh, what a slut."

"Don't you think it's very bad to talk about her like that?" Hwee Leng asked acidly.

"It's true what! She had sex on a pool table. At a party. People saw it. I'm not making anything up. And I don't find her face attractive, is that a crime?"

"Doesn't mean you have to be so insulting about it. How is it even your business?"

"Please lah," Ming Wei laughed in disbelief. "Like you never talk about who is with who, who breaks up with who?"

"Come on, that's obviously different—"

"But it's true what. And it's not like it's top secret or what. If it's such a big deal to her to have people talk about it, then she shouldn't do it, right? In public leh."

Trounced, Ming Wei thought, well and truly trounced. You could see it in her face, teetering on the edge of tantrum. So much about Hwee Leng to detest, but this emotionalism was the sour icing on the cake: if she couldn't stand the heat, she shouldn't pick fights. At the very least she could learn to recognise when she'd been beaten, and to shut up. But no, the self-righteous harangue just wouldn't stop—

"What if she hears the kind of words you use to talk about her? If it was me, I'd be really upset."

"Are you stupid enough to have sex on a pool table? In front of ten softball players? No? Then it's no problem lorh. Don't be so stupid, can already."

"It's mean." But she had no better comeback than that—she never did. And yet Andrew deferred endlessly to her killjoy whining. It was making his company unbearable. How long would it take him to wake up?

It had been a mistake, Ming Wei thought, to get dragged along to watching this today. He didn't have anything against debating—there was usually a *zai* character or two on the Ashford team, even if only in that gabby arts student way, sometimes separated from mere wordy bullshit by the finest of lines. But everyone knew the only match really worth the time was the annual final, which could be relied upon to pit Ashford against traditional rivals King Albert. This lot was just fodder.

Nothing about the hour to come changed his mind. The first speaker from Marine Parade, a stiff-kneed girl flapping tattered sheets of foolscap, stuttered mechanically through her material before sitting down, flustered, with three unused minutes on the clock. Ming Wei couldn't hold back a chuckle. "Watch out, it's the robot invasion! But she's like an anti-Transformer lah—less than meets the eye." She was succeeded by a neat, smiling Ashford boy whose understated urbanity came across as even smoother than usual.

"Wah, this is damn painful, man," Ming Wei said gleefully. "Massacre! Look at the next guy—" Here he referred to the unfortunate Chinh, glowering over his notes. "—the midget, sure he is in JC or not? Looks like forty years old like that. And check out his face, he looks like a serial killer. Sorry, man," he turned to Brian, "but Marine Parade got any normal people or not? Someone dumping radioactive waste in your canteen, is it, then all come out like that? Teenage Mutant Junior College."

Hwee Leng leaned across Andrew. "Will you stop it? It's not funny."

"Aiyah, don't so ngeow lah. Are you having PMS or what?"

"Hey, let's just watch the debate," Andrew said.

Ming Wei rolled his eyes.

Hwee Leng burned in anger for the rest of the match. She couldn't say a word about Ming Wei's behaviour toward herself—though annoying, it was, ultimately, nothing extraordinary, expressing nothing she didn't have to hear each day, in sly and stifled giggles, among her family and in her school. She'd long learned to sublimate these constant aggravations into her personal atmospheric mix; so that they appeared to the onlooker to vanish, while in fact they fed the invisible layers of disquiet that enveloped her, and that moved as she moved. She could absorb this sort of abuse, she sometimes thought, bottomlessly. Only injustice toward others precipitated her latent feelings into solid rage.

This wasn't altruism, but strategic instinct. Part public relations manoeuvre, part self-protective cloaking. She was on surer ground, with herself and with others, as long as she wasn't the victim. It would be too draining, and leave her too vulnerable, otherwise. She'd understood for longer than she could remember that it had to be that way.

Ming Wei, on the other hand, was borne aloft on a rising wave of amusement. It was mostly amusement. He would have called it amusement. But as it crashed and swept away, it left a flinty deposit of irritation in its wake.

The speech by Chinh, the small angry-looking weirdo, was an obvious disaster: he accepted seven interjections from the Ashford team, three times as many as usual, so that his opponents spoke for almost as much of his allotted time as he did. A performance so risible merited more than the few small snorts and murmurs to which Ming Wei confined himself, but Andrew met even these restrained offerings with polite stonewalling, while his girlfriend's eyes flashed reproach.

She had no sense of humour at all. People like that were fortunately few in number, but they really got under Ming Wei's skin. It showed a deplorable self-importance, an arrogant determination to put oneself above others. In Ming Wei's books, a refusal to laugh was a good barometer of character. Fun was serious business.

On one level, though, it was only to be expected that Hwee Leng would deny the objective crapness of her own team. Perhaps it was natural that those of little ability should be defensive about the whole idea of having standards. More troubling was Andrew's capitulation to her self-deception, even as the pathetic hilarity unfolding before them vindicated Ming Wei in every way. Just how low would Andrew stoop? Was there no limit to what he would play along with?

Ming Wei began to wonder if this relationship was not merely, as he had previously assumed, a temporary lapse on his friend's part—the type of entanglement that resulted if you were awkward or inexperienced around girls, and you compromised your pride for a bit, because easy release for your dick offered itself for little effort. That was embarrassing enough, of course, and, contemplating it, Ming Wei had been embarrassed on Andrew's behalf; but now he suspected the truth might be even worse. Maybe this acquiescence to Hwee Leng, to her overtures and her strictures, revealed some more fundamental bedrock defect in Andrew, some essential wishy-washiness, that Ming Wei had been too ready to overlook. Perhaps her repulsiveness was no accident. Perhaps Andrew really did agree with the bitch.

Ming Wei cast a furtive, appraising look at Andrew, who sat to his left; and then at the insipid identical brother on his other side. This new view of Andrew was both disappointing and oddly liberating. Andrew's achievements remained what they were, of course; in terms of academic and general social success he was no less a symbol of *zai*. But the connections Andrew chose went unavoidably to who he was. This flaccid deference before mediocrity, this cloying *refusal to judge*, mashing the solid world and its honest realities into a tepid porridge of cringing blandness, was a perversion, a failure of standards, and it diminished him, at the core, in a darkly irreparable way. The coarsely pragmatic might disagree, and say his sex life was his own business, but you could take pragmatism too far, Ming Wei thought.

On balance, it made sense to stay on the right side of him. Andrew was still a credit to him, a friend worth having. But perhaps the moral of the story was to be careful about admiring anyone. What seemed like the safest person could have the most damning personal weaknesses. Ming Wei would save his loyalty for his standards and where they would get him—which was, in any case, where it should always have been.

If he was honest about it, his hero thing for Andrew had never just been about his friend's merits, genuine and substantial though those were. It also had roots, Ming Wei knew, in his insecurities about his own background. Ashford and the Gifted Education Programme were full of guys who lived in large detached houses in pricey District 10. Each day they stepped out into the school foyer from the leather seats of air-conditioned BMWs or Mercedes Benzes, sometimes driven by chauffeurs; and every July and January, after the long school holidays, they swapped accounts of their sophisticated trips to London, Tokyo, Paris, Los Angeles. They spoke matter-of-factly of weekends in the swimming pools and on the tennis courts of private country clubs. Girls whispered about them with an undercurrent of excitement. Rightly or wrongly, being rich put you—effortlessly, talentlessly—several rungs up the ladder of *zai*.

Ming Wei both resented these guys and despised himself for it. The results of differences in wealth, like those in intelligence or beauty, were the textbook type of unfairness—bald and unarguable and entirely rational—about which he considered it petulant to complain. One should know one's value and one's place; and he did not exempt himself from this maxim. Nevertheless the question of money hurt him. In the Ashfordian scheme of things, the only scheme that mattered, he saw himself on the struggling end of the spectrum. He lived in private housing too, but it was only a flat in an old condominium estate, badly in need of renovation, without its own swimming pool. Unable to afford the latest SEGA machine, he made do with a knockoff console, preloaded with Nintendo games of dubious legality. He had never been further than Bangkok.

And needless to say, unlike spoiled kids like Hwee Leng,

to study overseas he would have to pay for the government's financial assistance with the first six years of his professional life. A scholarship was prestigious, to be sure, and well worth having—but only if you couldn't get abroad without one. It hadn't escaped Ming Wei's notice that the bungalow guys and the country club girls eschewed the common chatter about Ministries and statutory boards and government-linked corporations. Asked about the future, they gave non-committal shrugs and spoke of "going into business" or "keeping their options open". They planned for jobs in investment banks, law firms, multinationals. For more of what they already had. For money.

Ming Wei was headed for the consolation prize. He would not pass Go, or collect $200. He was on the loser track.

Elevating Andrew, he recognised, had taken some of the sting out of this. Ming Wei had indulged in a romance: a romance about a boy from a HDB flat coming to Ashford, a house of pure contest, and using pure ability to best the privileged at the game of life. A romance about the innate virtue of being a loser. It was so obviously stupid, now that he thought about it. Sure, Andrew was doing pretty well—considering he could do no better. The fastest horse on the sucker's course. But that couldn't change the hard truth about where he was—which was also where Ming Wei was—and it was useless fantasy to imagine otherwise.

He ought to be glad for this Hwee Leng affair, really,

for exposing his own lazy and sentimental investment in such magical bullshit thinking.

At least there wouldn't be long to go now before the debate ended and they were released from this tedious hell. He gave another sidelong glance at Andrew, who was a picture of earnest attention as the final Marine Parade speaker delivered an enthusiastic argument. Ming Wei would concede that this one had more of a brain than her teammates, and there was nothing immediately offensive in her appearance, but boy, did she have a screechy voice. Leaning toward Andrew, he released a high, thin wail in imitation. "Not bad huh, Indian also can sing Teochew opera."

"What I don't understand," Hwee Leng said, stabbing at the mound of shaved ice with her spoon, "is why you're friends with him at all."

Ming Wei had left them half an hour ago, with the parting words "Yah, yah, whatever" for her and "See you later, man" for Andrew, and still she had a bee in her bonnet about him. Not unreasonably, Andrew supposed, carefully folding bits of basil seed into his own bowl of ice. He never really minded Ming Wei's remarks himself, but he could see that they took some getting used to, and that going on about Marine Parade in that way might rankle if it were your school. "I agree he went too far today."

"Not just today. He's horrible to people!"

"He's just too blunt lah. But that is good also, in a way—you know where you stand with him."

"He's mean," Hwee Leng said, with another stab. "His whole way of seeing things, it's mean and—small. And it's not like he's stupid, or incapable of thinking differently. He's *deliberately* small."

"I think he's just saying what a lot of people are thinking."

"Maybe, but that's no reason to say them too. The whole world can be wrong about something, we don't have to go and follow them."

"No. No, we don't. You're right. But he isn't always so bad lah." He knew it wasn't entirely true, though, even as he said it. Ming Wei was a constant, a dependable quantity, as far as people could be. His brand of levity just didn't seem so crass when Hwee Leng wasn't around, her livewire consciousness saturating the air like an ion stream, charging the world with meanings Andrew didn't otherwise catch.

"Do you trust him? I mean, would you? With a secret or something, something really private, something that could really hurt you?"

Andrew hesitated. Until recently the question would have made little sense to him. He didn't go in for secrets or sharing, both portents of a kind of mess that he avoided by instinct. But now, without wanting to, with the memory chest of his guilty nights sunk somewhere deep in chains, he knew what she meant.

"I don't think so," he said after a while. "But—you can't trust everyone you know in that way, right? And you have to get along even with people you don't trust."

"You don't have to be friends with them."

This, again, was a foreign idea. Why not be friends with someone? Approaches, praise, deference and admiration: this had been Andrew's experience of other people, and it had never done him any harm. The lottery of labels had fallen in his favour; being with his peers had never come at the price of joining in laughter at someone who looked or sounded like him. Approval was his balmy natural habitat, outside of which lay danger without bounds. He homed toward approval with something between the magnetic instinct of a migratory bird and the strict cautious foresight of the chess player. Accretions to his identity—his sensibility, his interests and his desires—were meticulously trimmed to a kind of bonsai perfection, so that he seemed to conform quite organically to the world's demands. If he had been born with nothing that denied him inclusion, he had also never denied it to himself out of a commitment to something that didn't fit.

"Like that," he said. "There might not be many people to be friends with left."

"No," Hwee Leng said. "Maybe not. Isn't that an awful thought, though? That we're surrounded by people we'd call friends, who can't be trusted. Doesn't it make you sad?"

Perhaps it was sad, in theory. But how sad could it be? It

didn't touch the perfect geometry of his plans, those open roads ahead.

They ate for a while in silence. The sun was starting its heavy descent, spilling hot red gold across the sky.

"I've been thinking," Hwee Leng said. "About what you told me the other day."

The thought of Kevin, unbidden, tightened around Andrew like a fist. No, no, he thought. No. "What?"

"You know, what you said at Sentosa." The fist squeezed. "About that guy, the Year One, the one people were bullying."

"Oh yeah, that."

"I get that he didn't want you to tell anyone about it," Hwee Leng said. "And of course if that's what he says, then you can't. But I can't stop thinking that it's terrible for the classmates to just get away with it. I mean, it's a kind of—of molest, right?" Embarrassed by the subject, she didn't notice the strain that collected in Andrew's face before he smoothed it, with an iron will, away. "So I thought, maybe you should try to persuade him to go to a teacher. You could even say that you'll go with him, for, like, moral support. I guess you have to be careful how you do it, you don't want to push him if he's uncomfortable, but it could be that to him it doesn't look like an option right now, to do anything about it, but if there's someone behind him, then it will seem…possible."

Scattered ice floes and slivers of jelly remained in the cold syrup of Andrew's bowl. Also the white oval piece of attap chee, hard and translucent, he had been saving for last. He pushed these bits around gratefully—it gave him time, he thought, to work this out—but it was no help, he could not think under these conditions, with Hwee Leng's face turned toward him, bright and expectant. Above all he needed to see the matter with Kevin the way she did—the way he had communicated it to her, in that seaside moment of absolution. If he lost that meagre trail of crumbs he was out in the wilderness on his own. But he was afraid of where her call to action might take him—blundering into contact with Kevin, entanglement, intimacy—and it made him afraid that he was afraid. This was dangerous, these thoughts, they would catch him in a hall of mirrors. He needed a response that would make sense on her terms. She was still watching him. He could not think.

"I don't really know the guy," he said. "I mean, I don't know him very well. I don't know if I should just anyhow bring this up again. It's a sensitive thing and it might be—kind of busybody."

"Well, he obviously felt he could bring it up with you."

He took a steadying breath. "That's—true—but then it's been quite some time already, since it happened. Half the June holidays already. Maybe it's better if he can just move on. Who knows, maybe he is already getting over it, and if I mention it again, it might just make things worse for him."

Hwee Leng, picking at her lower lip, considered this

perspective for a while. Andrew watched her credulously placing his counterfeit concern on the scales, among her own true weights, and felt a creeping shame. This was no good. His feeble, scrambling insincerity undermined whatever it was meant to defend; it was itself an admission that he had something to hide.

"I can see why it might be awkward," she was saying now. "And I can see why—well, I'm not surprised—you'd feel weird about doing it. But he had faith enough in you to talk about it the last time. I guess you're right that you should make it clear from the start, you won't push if he'd rather just leave it alone. But it doesn't sound like it's wrong to even mention it at all. From what you've said, I think he'll recognise that it's not out of malice or you being kaypoh or anything, it's just—an offer to be there if he wants it. I'm sure he'll see where you're coming from."

Where exactly am I coming from? Andrew wondered hopelessly. Perhaps she was wrong, and perhaps she was right, but he wasn't in a place to think sensibly about why. Because he couldn't trust his own rejections of her analysis, he felt himself tilting, with fatalistic illogic, toward agreement. He would do it, because he had to prove to himself that he could.

"I can see what you're saying," he said quietly. "I mean, it's a good idea."

Hwee Leng was surprised and pleased. She habitually formed schemes of this nature, always without takers: she'd tried for months, without success, to get Brian to get Ravi to ease up on Chinh. "I'm glad you think so. I really think someone has to be there for him, as a sort of—matter of conscience—and it sounds like there might not be anyone else." Andrew nodded through all this, with a crooked attempt at a smile. "I appreciate it's not easy," she went on, trying for softness, now that she'd won. "Especially when it's not someone you know well. It's great of you to do it. It's a difficult thing to do."

"Difficult," he repeated. "But the right thing."

"Exactly." She beamed at him. "And I keep thinking, no matter how difficult it is for you to offer to help, it has to be a thousand times harder to be him."

Andrew could not go as far as that. He was at the limits of his charade. He ran a hand up across his face, and back through his hair, so that for just a few moments he could block out the sight of her and the need for speech.

He told himself later that perhaps it did not matter too much what he said he'd do. He had no clue how to locate Kevin: he didn't know the other boy's class or his faculty, or which teams or clubs he might have joined. He wasn't even sure of his last name. There was no reason, in the ordinary course of things, why they would meet; and with two weeks left in the June break, a chance encounter was unlikely to take place soon. So it was entirely possible that Hwee Leng would forget about the whole affair before he was in any position to follow up on his word, although he suspected (correctly) that she didn't generally forget such things. It was also possible—of course, why not?—that Andrew himself would forget, and that would be the end of that. It could all be carried away, fluttering, by a breeze: this oddly fraught evening conversation, its idle speculations on a stranger, the other boy's shoulder blades and forearms and soft dark hair. Pond skaters across the surface of his life. Vanishing into the grass. In the meantime it was no big deal, one student lending support to another, just a dry matter of conscience, as Hwee Leng had said. She was a persuasive girl, after all; and he had been, he told himself, persuaded.

If such thoughts did not grant Andrew serenity, they at least pulled the world around him into flat, manageable planes; and he succeeded in confining his feeling of impending threat to a few well-defined blocks of time. In these airless moments, he knew he was going to have to give something up, although he couldn't say what it would be, and everything, everything, seemed non-negotiable if he was to be safe. But after ten minutes, fifteen at most, grimly, determinedly, he jerked these freefalls of emotion to a halt, and returned to the spartan efficiency of his functional routines.

He said less and less to Hwee Leng, without realising it.

A number of major badminton matches appeared on the horizon and he gratefully scheduled a punishing series of practice sessions in response. Within the tidy white rectangles of the court his objectives were clear, his communications bounded. Off it, before and after, he submitted easily to the clockwork predictability of Ming Wei's cynicism—a quality which made his company undemanding, if not precisely pleasant. Once or twice Andrew felt a sneaking sympathy for his complaints about Hwee Leng. There was something to be said for not being asked to think.

On an afternoon about a week later, Ming Wei, buoyed by his friend's partial return to the fold, was especially garrulous. "Sorry, man," he said excitedly as they limbered up on the court. "Can't stick around later. Got to meet this Year One chio bu. You know that Jennifer Chong? Med fac girl, quite flat-chested lah, but damn nice legs. She needs help with binomial expansions, they are *so* hard—" He flapped his wrists to affect his idea of feminine confusion. "—and you know I'm the ultimate gentleman, right? Especially if you have such great legs." He paused, calculating how much he could get away with. "You should try it out, man, make use of your capital. You're hot currency! There are so many cute chicks waiting to be impressed."

"Aiyah, who has the time?" Andrew gave a pained smile and went on stretching. Part of him felt he ought to protest this erasure of Hwee Leng, but he hadn't the stomach to fight any fights today. All he wanted was to play some badminton.

They took up their usual stances beside each other, mirrored on the other side of the net by their teammates Choon Keong and Halim. After a few lukewarm rallies they began in earnest, and Andrew trimmed the beam of his attention down to the play—the intricate series of arcs weaved by the shuttlecock through the air, swooping and diving across thirteen by six metres of space, a superficially random result generated by the interlocking of four strategic minds. As the game flowed through him, he felt a powerful relief. He had always known this and, he could feel sure, he always would. He was eighteen years old, obliviously strong, and his mind would not go as far as the illness or accident or plain old age that might rob him of it. The darting dance of forecourt, midcourt, rearcourt, and the swift and controlled applications of arm and wrist, were firmly and unassailably his.

Twenty minutes in, a rapid exchange of strokes crescendoed into a dramatic smash; and Andrew, exhilarated, wiping runs of fresh sweat from his forehead with a white cotton sleeve, looked up toward one of the wide open lengths of the hall and caught sight of a familiar frame. It was Kevin, leaning against a pillar, watching them play. He wore the clean look of new-cut hair, and his face was thoughtful and composed in the soft afternoon sun.

Sport had set a steady fire going in Andrew's muscles and made him expansive. He smiled at Kevin, and Kevin smiled back. He was just a guy he knew. Of course Andrew could offer him a hand, as Hwee Leng had suggested. Probably he wouldn't want it—and that would be it, case closed—but he would appreciate the gesture, one person to another. They could pass like this, and smile at each other, and it would all be natural, matter-of-fact.

He played on, giving no further outward attention to their audience of one, although the inner coil of him glowed with secret contentment. As the game wound down—Andrew and Ming Wei won—he cast a quick glance at the spot. It was vacant now, but no matter, he told himself dizzily, no matter. The four players moved to the changing room together, in a swirl of noisy chatter: reviewing an early rally, dissecting a skilful, unexpected save. Andrew floated easy contributions into this talk, all the while looking back on the past hour in the warm double light of the hidden chambers of his heart.

Perhaps he need give nothing up, after all.

Then he heard Ming Wei, as he pulled a clean shirt on: "—that was freaky, man, staring at us, I kept wondering when he would go away."

"Who?" Andrew asked.

"Aiyoh, you mean you didn't see? Sometimes you really are a blur king." The others chortled. "This ah kua from Year One spent the whole match ogling at us, that, what, Kelvin Teng—"

"Kevin Cheng," Halim corrected.

"Yah, yah, okay, whatever, I'm not an expert on the exotic world of the Ashford homos, but obviously Halim is. Why so interested in them ah?" Ming Wei crossed his arms across his chest in a gesture of exaggerated protectiveness. "Shit, man, I got change in front of you how many times already some more."

"Don't anyhow say lah, my excuse very solid one—this guy is in my sister's class, that's how come I heard of him before. He is one hundred percent psycho. Always breaking down over crazy things."

"I heard his classmates gave him a hard time." Andrew said it before he could stop himself.

"Oh, yes," Halim said, with the knowingness of gossip.

"What? What?" Ming Wei demanded. "Don't just give us this oh, yes, oh, yes—what's the story!"

"It was one of those—surprise birthday celebrations. Some of the guys got him a present—some deep heat. And helped him to apply it—you know—" Halim, eyebrows raised, pointed to his crotch.

The other two howled, half in delight and half in disgust.

"That's damn horrible," Choon Keong said, between chuckles. "Wahlau eh. You got to feel sorry for the guy. Even if he's psycho. Deep heat on the little brother—ow!"

"To you lah," Ming Wei countered. "But this guy is a homo, remember? He probably liked it. Ask your sister to ask the guys lah, Halim. I'm sure they can tell us that he liked it."

More laughter. Andrew shivered. He made a surreptitious scan of the three mirthful faces. None of them had yet noticed him here, outside, complicit, unlaughing, unsafe. He had been lucky, but he could not count on it to last if he did not regain control of himself. He curled his hands into fists to keep them steady. He schooled his face into a blank. He had to be vigilant. There were too many opportunities to make irreversible mistakes.

They vanished: Ming Wei sloping off eagerly to his meeting in the canteen, the other two melting away into the late afternoon. Clouds sat fat and low in the sky and the wind carried the moist smell of coming rain. Andrew, peering out at the spread of grey, wondered if he could make it to the bus stop in time. Probably his chances were best if he left right away.

He had just stepped out through the school gates onto the street when he heard the slap of running shoes on the paved ground behind him. Even before the shouts of "Hey! Hey!" he knew, with a curious mix of dull excitement and fatalistic dread, who it would be.

"You going home?" Kevin asked, slowing to match him.

"Yeah."

"I don't know anything about badminton, but that looked exciting."

Andrew regretted the smile, the invitation to contact,

which he could not now disclaim. Every instant in this boy's presence was an error. How to make him go away? His mind turned, dissolutely, to excuses—he had left a book behind, he had forgotten an appointment. Kevin walked by his side with a kind of bounce in his gait, a rustling energy, and the novelty of his cheerfulness confused Andrew. He looked briefly at the other boy's profile—the dark fans of his eyelashes, the line of the bone in his jaw—and then he looked away, his throat closing. He could not regret the smile.

"We've got some big games when school re-opens. So we're training pretty hard."

Speaking magnified the error; but it would only be a short walk together, along a limited way, Andrew told himself, and then (and something in him fluttered in protest at the thought) it would be over forever.

"Even during holidays! I was in school for orchestra practice."

"What do you play?"

"Clarinet. But I'm not very good."

Andrew didn't know anything about music beyond what they'd had to do in school, perfunctorily, for an hour or so a fortnight. Mostly this had involved graceless mechanical puffing on hollow wooden recorders. But some of the equipment had interested him, vaguely, with its intimations of mathematics. In their shadow Kevin seemed both more solid and more unknown.

"Have you got—a concert, or something?"

"Yah, all the time, but every year the big one is in August."

The first bus stop they came to ran in the wrong direction for Andrew—he had to cross an overhead bridge to board from the other side of the dual carriageway. He had no idea where Kevin was headed, and with that odd double feeling in his gut again, a compound of alarm and relief, he thought they might already have to part. There was a moment's hovering, an exchange of looks, and then without words both continued toward the stairs up to the bridge.

Thunder rumbled but they took the steps unhurriedly. At the top their way along the concrete path was lined on either side by planter boxes filled with the deep rich pink of bougainvilleas. A daily route turned strangely ceremonial. Andrew divided it into portions: they would walk the whole length of the bridge together, they would walk more than half, they had half left, a quarter, five steps, now the descent. There would be a wait for the bus. Two minutes or twenty. Either of them might go first. They might need the same one. He did not want to jinx it, whatever that meant, by asking.

There was no one else at the bus stop. They stood, loosely facing each other. Andrew longed for the silence to go on, just to go on, but Kevin was trying to speak.

"I never thanked you," he said. "For, like, listening to me. The last time. About the guys in my class."

The last thing Andrew wanted was context, crowding round. He made a non-committal sound.

"You were nice about it. Lots of people wouldn't be. I—I have a friend," Kevin continued, hesitantly, and then, with a kind of sad calm, he told Andrew the brief and anonymous story of Leila's encounter with Samuel de Souza.

At first Andrew struggled to listen. It was both too distant and too raw: it had to do with someone else, not him, not them; and it was too much to do with that person, the account was composed of items too visceral to be neutrally shared at such a remove. The dirty language of violence and of shame. This nameless girl should have gone quietly, he felt. A bad idea to speak, to offer herself up to be mangled coldly and bloodily between the gears of the way things were done. A bad idea, too, to tell Kevin, who was now telling Andrew—and who knew who else would sup on her pain, pinning her open at the skin to probe and rootle inside. Each word a further greasy grinding of flesh, and it was out there now, she could never recall it or keep it back.

"So I think it was lucky I talked to you," Kevin said, simply, at the end. "I guess it wasn't only luck lah, you were nice to me before, but still—" he shrugged. "—if I went to this teacher instead…"

And Andrew had meant, at least in theory, to urge him to do just that. More—he had agreed to volunteer, to place his own body between Kevin and an order that was without mercy. For what purpose? So that they could be destroyed together, in some weird and sickly gesture? Far from her sustaining force, Hwee Leng's imperative logic unravelled. Remembering her made Andrew feel ill.

He hadn't really looked Kevin full in the face once during their entire conversation. He did so now. The other boy had pulled the cross he wore on a chain up to his chin, and was picking at it unconsciously, jamming its bottom edge into the skin under his fingernails. The hard white of his teeth peeked out from between his lips. Andrew formed, for the first time in his life, the clear thought that he would very much like to kiss him. And the clear thought that he must never do such a thing.

This was it, he thought. The bargain. He had to give this up to have the rest. He had been promised the safe, shining fields of the future, and they did not come without a price.

He pulled back quickly, standing straighter. "I'm sorry that you have problems," he said stiffly. "But I can't make them mine."

Kevin looked puzzled. "I just wanted to thank—to say—"

Andrew, with the perfect clarity of panic, willed as much coldness into his stance and his voice as he could. "And I don't think you should tell me about these problems of your friend. I can't help you. Sorry."

The other boy stared at him in openly hurt silence. If he couldn't parse the sense of Andrew's words, he grasped their tone well enough. The confusion in his eyes lodged in Andrew like a dagger.

Behind Andrew came the rasping engine of a bus. He hadn't noticed it rolling up, but he felt an immediate and painful burst of gratitude. He couldn't bring himself to any niceties—"This is my bus", or "I have to go", or a plain goodbye—none of them would add anything. There was nothing to add. He turned away from Kevin and fled, up the broad single step through the waiting door, into the vehicle's dim and empty refuge. Habit took over with its blessed automatic magic: he bought a ticket, steadied his feet, climbed the stairs, and moved as he always did, toward the front, to take a seat. It was only a few minutes later, as plush drops of rain finally shattered against the window, washing the world outside into watercolour waves, that he realised that he and his fellow passengers were churning down an unfamiliar street. He was on the wrong bus entirely.

When Brian came home from the first day of term, a week or so later, Andrew was sitting in their room in his usual working position: leaning earnestly forward, his left arm forming an L, fingers propping his forehead and elbow on the desk. His right hand skimmed quietly over the pages of a book. He looked freshly washed.

Brian slung his bag into its customary spot by his side of the bed. Ordinarily he would busy himself at the closet, preparing wordlessly for a shower of his own. But he had just spent much of the day, between lessons, with Hwee

Leng, talking his brother over—or, perhaps more accurately, offering awkward companionship as she contemplated Andrew, silently and not-so-silently, tearfully and not-so-tearfully. Facing Andrew himself, after hours of this, it seemed odd to now say nothing at all.

On the other hand, saying nothing at all, whatever the circumstances, was their established mode of shared existence. It felt almost like what this room was for.

He compromised on saying just a little.

"Hey, er—Hwee Leng told me—you know, about you guys."

Andrew turned round very slowly. He looked unperturbed. "Yeah." He paused. "Is she okay?"

Brian sat on the bed. "Er—actually—not very good lah. She was quite unhappy today."

"I hope she's not pissed off at me."

"I don't think so lah. She says it's up to you—if that's how it is for you, then it's better than wasting everybody's time. She's just, you know, upset."

Andrew sighed. "I feel bad about it," he said. "She's great, you know. There's nothing *wrong* with her or anything. There's nothing wrong with any of it. I just don't really… I mean, I'm sorry that she's upset, but I just—don't really want to go on."

Brian nodded. "Yah. Sometimes it's just like that. It's normal lah."

"Is it really?" His brother's voice was bitter.

"Yah, I mean, aiyah, this happened to me too. You can't help it, you—you like someone or you don't like someone, it's just like that. Can't really explain these things with logic or what. Don't worry about it lah. She gets it."

They were silent for a while.

"I hope it's not weird for you," Andrew said.

"Me?"

"Yeah, I mean, you guys are friends and all that, I hope that isn't—affected—by this."

"Oh, no lah," Brian said, surprised. "It's fine."

"Good," his brother said. This last loose end resolved, he began to collect himself to return to work. "Thanks for—for the talk."

"No problem. Are you okay?"

"Yeah. Thanks. I'm fine." He turned away, back into the world of his books.

Brian took his clothes to the shower with the thought that the exchange had been much less uncomfortable than he had feared. He didn't know if he had succeeded in reassuring his brother at all, but on balance, he felt it was better to have brought it up than not. As he unbuttoned his shirt it occurred to him that this was the first time they had ever had a conversation of such a personal sort. He wondered if it would take them quite so long to get around to the next.

# MARCH 1998

Only the shrapnel of the event, scattered bits and pieces, made it to Brian over the telephone; and they came in no very organised fashion at that. But this is what happened.

The first that Hwee Leng heard of it was at the SingSoc bop on at Christ's College. "A bop is a kind of shitty Cambridge student disco," she offered by way of explanation, which still left Brian mostly in the dark, but he didn't want to interrupt more than strictly necessary. She usually gave SingSoc social events a miss, "because it's always the same smug Ashford scholar lot, who all know each other from junior college; they spend all their time in Cambridge hanging out with other Singaporeans, talking about how backward and inefficient England is, and they'll all go back and mingle incestuously in the civil service, thinking they've now seen the world—you know what I mean." (Brian didn't really.) As it turned out, her boyfriend Dilip had resolved to patch a leak in his thesis that night, and kicked her out of his room, grumbling, close to midnight. Since she hadn't made other plans, and

Dilip lived more or less next door to Christ's, Hwee Leng decided to drop by.

She hoped partly, in fact, to catch up with Andrew, whom she hadn't seen for—it must have been months. It had occurred to her lately that he was soon embarking on his last term, after which he would fly home and begin a glittering ascent through Singapore's administrative elite; whereas she, if all went to plan, would spend several more years in a cold rented room somewhere in England, living on pasta and tinned tomatoes, while somehow producing enough words, reflecting enough thought, to amount to a doctorate. She wanted to meet Andrew on the same plane, in the same space, before their lives diverged with such finality. (This was how she framed it for herself, at any rate. There was something artificial about the idea: functionally, their friendship was limited to a handful of chats a term at best. They were not close. But Hwee Leng had too much self-regarding nostalgia to let that interfere with the set piece in her head.)

It was a typical night in early March: essentially still crystal cold, but brighter for longer, and those precious extra minutes of evening sun left gentle hints of spring in the air, so that you could risk a short walk without hat or gloves. Even so, Hwee Leng was glad to make it past the chilly old stone college courtyards, and step into the heated mouth of the 1960s concrete building that housed the bop.

There weren't many people in the entrance hall as

she peeled off her heavy brown coat and the red fleece underneath. A few SingSoc committee members—Ashleigh, Gaurav and Ming Wei ("You remember him, don't you?")—huddled animatedly over a table. The wooden surface was covered with small square scraps of paper, a cluster of empty beer and alcopop bottles, and the ubiquitous white plastic cups from which students knocked back bad wine and unpalatably strong parodies of mixed drinks. When the three noticed Hwee Leng their voices dropped spontaneously into a shared hush of excitement, and they fixed her with a curious stare that she only partially registered at the time. (It was not exactly unusual enough to draw her attention; if she was happy here at university, it wasn't because her compatriots sniggered at her any less than they had ever done.) Gaurav swung open the little black metal box in front of him and eased it round to face her. "It's a pound, madam!" he announced theatrically.

Hwee Leng fished her wallet from her jeans and dropped the entry fee in with a clang. "How's it going?"

"Good," Ming Wei said. "And you?"

"Yeah, not bad."

"It's been quite an exciting night," Ashleigh said, her rouged face flushed redder with drink. "Don't you think?" She tittered and almost slipped off her seat. Hwee Leng raised her eyebrows and gave a thin smile. This was more conversation than she was ordinarily deemed to merit.

She knew that Ashleigh had christened her—among other things—"that spotty bulldog bitch". Presumably it was the alcohol being friendly tonight. Hwee Leng turned and made her way into the darkness of the bop proper, as Gaurav jabbed his giggling friend in the ribs.

There were no surprises here. Loose, overlapping circles of figures, bobbing and swaying, were lit up, poorly and periodically, by the repetitive red-green-blue of cheap party lights. The air was filled with the undemanding comfort of four-four beats and lyrics everyone knew, or learned in seconds, even if only involuntarily. People posed, and watched, and swigged mouthfuls from bottles; a few, more ambitious, made shouted attempts at conversation in irregular pockets of the room. In her early undergraduate days, Hwee Leng had dutifully painted her face (a task for which she had neither skill nor enthusiasm), and pulled on too-tight clothes and tottery shoes, to endure far more such evenings than she liked to remember. All part of the experience, she had told herself at the time. This is what you do here. Don't miss out. She was more willing to admit it these days: this stuff bored her stiff.

Where was Andrew? As the SingSoc Treasurer he was ordinarily a reliable fixture at socials. She didn't recognise any of the younger students, and she wasn't really in the mood to meet new people. She was beginning to regret the wasted pound when she sighted Karen in a corner, sitting in a semicircle of similarly skinny girls wearing sleek identikit haircuts. Hwee Leng didn't know the others, but she and Karen had shared lectures in their first year, swapping cordial enough observations on the material. Someone to chat to for a bit, at least. She hurried over to the table.

"Hey."

"Oh, hey." Karen looked up.

"How is everything?"

"Not bad. How's the thesis going?"

Hwee Leng made a face. "It isn't, really. Going, that is. You know how it is."

Karen smiled. She offered brief introductions of the others at the table (the Cambridge standard, college and subject), which were incomprehensible over the din. Each nodded and smiled in turn, but they seemed disinclined to speak further, and Hwee Leng had the feeling she might be interrupting. Back to Plan A, then. "Have you seen Andrew?" she yelled.

"Andrew…?"

"Andrew Teo. Corpus Christi." There weren't any other Singaporean Andrews, were there? Some new undergraduate she hadn't yet met, perhaps. "Have you seen him?"

The unknown girls stirred, firing nervous looks at one another, and then returned to Hwee Leng with new attention. It reminded Hwee Leng of the cloth-spreading motion of a flock of birds, disturbed from a field into momentary flight. Karen frowned and bit her lip. "He was here earlier, but he left." She hesitated. "Do you want a drink?"

"I'm fine, thanks."

Karen nodded. After a second she opened her mouth as if to say more, and then shut it, and then seemed about to reconsider when the first notes of a squeaky Danish pop song—the universal soundtrack to all public spaces for some months now—pealed through the room, resolving the question for her. "Hey—" "Oh, yes—" "Come on—" Eagerness spilled through the table like a wave. The girls were all on their feet, headed for the dance floor. One tugged politely at Hwee Leng's arm, but she demurred, and they did not press her.

Alone, and mildly put out, Hwee Leng made another quick round of the room, keeping an eye out for Andrew. Perhaps Karen was wrong, and he was still here; but no, he wasn't, and she began to feel faintly ridiculous, circling a bop full of semi-strangers in pursuit of her ex-boyfriend. It was then that she noticed it, him, the face she was looking for, lying on an unoccupied table in the half-light near the door. What she had assumed to be a flyer for the bop, or some other event, was in fact a colour photocopy of a picture. Half a dozen more copies slumped near it on the floor.

She grabbed one square and ran out into the entrance hall to hold it up to the light. Yes, it was Andrew. Or Brian. Well, it must be Andrew. That explains a few things, a selfish part of her noted wryly—but then a dreadful idea crystallised, as she remembered the paper scattered on the ticket table, and she whirled round to have a look. The trio of SingSoc members, still there, drank in the view of her with undisguised glee. She lunged forward and put a hand to the stack of pictures on the wooden surface, another four or five, some stained burgundy with wine.

"What the hell is this?"

"Nobody knows," Gaurav said. "Maybe you can tell us. Who's the other guy, the ang moh?"

Ashleigh had to hide behind her silk turquoise shawl, she was shaking with so much silent laughter.

"You didn't know he was—that way—either?" Ming Wei asked. "We wondered, you know, because back in JC you were together and all that. Wah, this is even more shocking—"

Hwee Leng intended merely to shake her head, but her impatience swelled the motion to include her shoulders. "I couldn't give a shit about him being gay—" The word sent Ashleigh, behind shawl, into further paroxysms. "—I mean, what the hell is this?" She waved one of the pictures in their faces. "Why are there—these—things—all over the fucking place?"

"Somebody left them here," Ming Wei said. "Before the bop started."

"Who?"

Gaurav spread his hands. "Don't know. Must be the same person with the email."

"What email?"

"Didn't you get it too? Oh—but you're not a scholar.

Don't know who else got it."

"Check your email lah, probably you'll see it."

Hwee Leng's head began to spin with fury and confusion. "Where is Andrew?"

A shrug passed through the others. "He was here just now, but he left suddenly," Ming Wei said. "Not sure where. He didn't say. We had to stay to run the bop."

"Why the fuck—" —didn't you follow? —do you find this so funny? —would anyone do this to him? She started to shout all three things at once, but stopped herself. It was useless with these people. Worse than useless; they were loving it, siphoning and savouring all signs of distress, like it was a rare nectar. That was her answer right there, that was why someone would do this. A pleasure too great, it seemed, as she stared into their faces, for Ming Wei to even try to withstand.

"You asshole," she said to him. "Aren't you supposed to be *his friend*?"

Ming Wei gestured to the spread of photographs. "How was I supposed to know he'd be so stupid to get himself into this kind of position?"

Hwee Leng responded by snatching up the pictures, knocking aside cups and bottles to reach a few more.

"Hey, watch it!" Drink on cloth. "This is Chanel!"

Rage rushed through Hwee Leng. She deliberately pushed more bottles over, unleashing frantic cries from the others, before stamping to the black bin bag hanging from the edge of the table and thrusting the scraps of paper in. A moment later she had second thoughts. Better to be safe. So she reached into the sticky beery mess of the violently rustling bag, fished the pictures out, tore them into pieces, and dropped them back in again.

Then she returned to the other room and barrelled through the dance floor, shoving bodies aside without apology, gathering fistfuls of photographs as she went. She found them mostly clustered on and around the tables—it turned out she had been standing on a few while speaking to Karen—and in a minute or two she was done. People stared and pointed and shouted to one another (whispering was impossible in the blare of the synthesisers). Well, let them. She didn't care.

As she dumped the last of the loathsome collection into the bin bag, she became aware of someone touching her elbow gently. It was Karen.

"I wasn't sure should I tell you or not," she said in a small voice. "When you asked about him, I thought maybe you'd seen them already. Or the email."

This email again. "No. I have never seen any of this shit in my life. Do you know who did this?"

"No idea. Quite mean, right?"

*Quite mean.* But you did nothing. Drank and danced. Hwee Leng took a long slow breath, doing her best to hold back her contempt.

"Are you okay? I know..." Karen trailed off.

"Am *I* okay?" Red haze threatened Hwee Leng's vision. "Am *I* okay? What the—what does it have to do with—" She choked it back. Priorities. Information. She needed information. She tried, unsuccessfully, to keep her voice down. "Did you see him here earlier? Andrew?"

Karen hesitated, then nodded. "Yeah—" And she gave Hwee Leng a brief account. She had come by early in the evening, with some SingSoc committee members, to help set up for the bop. Initially the tables had been bare; but at some point, without anyone being able to say exactly how or when, while crates of drinks were carried, and lights were rigged and tested, and sound checks echoed through the rooms, the pictures had appeared everywhere at once, like some kind of toxic plankton bloom. The preparations halted in amazement, as people gathered and gaped around the table in the entrance hall; and it was into the middle of this shocked and swooning crowd that Andrew himself pushed when he arrived, completely unaware.

"It hit him pretty hard," Karen said. "He just kind of stood there and stared for a few seconds, and then he turned around and ran out."

"Didn't anyone go after him?" Hwee Leng didn't really expect an answer; and, sure enough, Karen merely spread her palms helplessly. "And this email thing—what's this email thing?"

"I don't really know. Huimin told me about it. She came a bit later, and she said she'd already seen the picture because it was in some email. I haven't seen it myself."

So it could actually get worse. Pity twisted in Hwee Leng's gut. She felt both that she desperately had to speak to Andrew, and that there was no good at all that it could do. But either way—she looked at the faces around her, some openly titillated, others embarrassed, and weakly attempting discretion—she had to get away from this gruesome theatre.

"Thanks, Karen," she said, pulling to leave.

"Are you okay?" Karen asked again.

She didn't answer, just got her coat and left.

"It was damn drama!" Ming Wei recounted to a bright-eyed group, standing in a half-circle in the cold, a few minutes later. He was buzzing with delight. "First time I ever saw something like that in my life, man. She was like a madwoman. Guess it must have been hard for her—her big high point in JC, the one time she scored so far out of her league, he turned out to be a homo!"

"It was damn bo sei, can?" Ashleigh said, taking a drag on her cigarette and tossing her fringe out of her eyes. She was still sour about her spill-soaked cardigan. "Okay lah, it's some super emotional moment for you, whatever, you can still have some dignity, right? You went out with a homo, that's one thing; don't need to embarrass yourself with a giant public meltdown some more."

"Bet she liked the attention. How else is she going to get any?"

"You have to feel sorry for her," Gaurav said with a chuckle. "What a way to find out."

Ashleigh smiled. "You know, I find it really funny that that Karen Soong and some of her friends were like, oh, it's so mean to spread the picture, it's so mean, it's his private business, all that. But when I look at the photo, all I can think is, man, that ang moh guy is so bloody ugly! Weedy, pasty, teeth all crooked—I mean, homo also can have standards, right?"

"Aiyah, what *mean*," Ming Wei said, annoyed. "Facts are facts, right? Seriously, man, I never thought Andrew would be so dumb. Want to be a pervert, okay lah, that's one thing, but don't go and take photos of yourself some more, and then later complain when of course other people find it scandalous. You take stupid risks, you got to accept you might get burned. That's just life, man." He took a drink from his bottle. "That's just life."

The wine was much better, and there were *hors d'oeuvres*, when the trio revisited the subject almost a decade later, at an invitation-only gathering of the young and upcoming among the establishment elite.

"This is not just about the narrow gay issue," Gaurav intoned. (He was making quite the name for himself, these days, in the Ministry of Finance.) "We wouldn't need to talk about it if it was just this single petition on a trivial law. Ultimately it doesn't really matter if gay sex is legal or not. More importantly, it's about managing the social rifts that result from the uneven effects of globalisation. Many of us in this room saw homosexuals when we were studying overseas, and to us it is not so shocking, but not everyone in Singapore has that level of exposure. We Cosmopolitans have to realise we are the minority; the attitudes are not the same—some might say not so enlightened—among the Heartlanders."

"I think it's very true, what you say about the social divide," Ashleigh said. (She was now a rising star in the lower divisions of the judiciary.) "But we shouldn't be so quick to stereotype the Heartlanders as backward: questions of values are inherently subjective, and the Cosmopolitan viewpoint is not always superior. We shouldn't blindly assume Western societies have the correct balance between individual freedom and social responsibility. Anyway, where does it stop? Today, change the Penal Code; tomorrow, they will want to adopt children. *Human rights—*" (she made air quotes with her fingers) "—may be the fashion in the West, but that doesn't mean they should trump everything else."

"I agree with you both," Ming Wei said. (Currently doing time in the Transport ministry, he desperately wanted a permanent place in this charmed circle. So far he had only managed to wheedle a colleague into bringing him as an occasional guest.) "What bothers me is the entitled tone of the gays, all this playing of the victim card." There was a lot of vigorous, knowledgeable nodding. "The government already said very clearly, many times, nobody goes to jail just for being homosexual. Nobody is stopping a homosexual from going to university, getting a job, working hard like the rest of us. So when they make all this noise about being oppressed, it's obviously not the real agenda. They're not happy just with having their private life; they want to push everyone else to celebrate their lifestyle, never mind if the rest of society is not ready, or not interested in hearing about what sex they have."

"That's a very good point," Ashleigh said. "They always talk about freedom and rights, but they don't give other people the freedom, the right, to have a different opinion from them. They talk about being open-minded, but they don't accept any questions about their own dogma. If you don't line up one hundred percent behind them, and say yes, whoo hoo, let's show *Brokeback Mountain* to primary school children, they make personal attacks on you."

"Exactly," Ming Wei said. "They don't let you talk about their AIDS problem—you mention AIDS and you are a bigot! And as some of us know from personal contact with them—" Here his voice dropped to convey a suitable solemnity. "—many homosexuals have other psychological problems too, mental instability, not family-oriented. But if you bring that up, any facts which conflict with their gay pride agenda, they brand you a homophobe."

Gaurav sighed. "The sad thing is, it only hurts their own cause, when they adopt such a confrontational, almost a hysterical, stance. Makes them seem like extremists, when they act like impatient screaming banshees, demanding change overnight. Nothing justifies incivility."

"It's so ironic," Ming Wei added cleverly, feeling pleased with his own performance, and optimistic about his chances of being asked back. "I think most of their problems come from their own behaviour. If they just kept quiet, instead of petitioning and promoting themselves so aggressively, society wouldn't feel the need to push back. Sometimes people are their own worst enemies."

They all agreed this was very true; and the conversation drifted on to higher things. Their wisdom was too urgently needed in other quarters to linger on such hopeless cases any longer.

Hwee Leng reached the front gate of Christ's at a trot, and then paused on the street to assess her next move, the roar of blood in her face somewhat cooled after a few seconds in the witching hour night. Something had to be done—but what? The most obvious option was to drop in on Andrew, but Hwee Leng didn't know where his room was exactly, though she had the impression it was back in the main college site this year. She wasn't sure whom she could ask. The Singaporeans at the bop were out of the question, and she suspected the dour college porters wouldn't look kindly upon such a request even in daylight, never mind at this time. She could call him; but her phone book was lying in the bottom desk drawer in her room—a good half hour's trek up the hill. And what if he was asleep? Karen's account placed the episode at Christ's at several hours ago. Might it not be a better idea to leave him to rest, and to check in on him in the morning?

This was all terribly unsatisfactory. She supposed she could take her chances at Corpus—some colleges put the names of students on their staircases. She would look absurd peering at them in turn, but she was used to that; and perhaps she would get lucky and find him near the front gate. In any case there was no point loitering here. Across the street loud drunks crammed a taxi rank. She hurried down Petty Cury, dodging the counterflow of scarfed and coated students, then wound rapidly past the Corn Exchange, glad that she had given up wearing heels in winter. It was getting colder now, the fading season asserting a last few hours of triumph, and as she came at last to the heavy, unfamiliar gates—Corpus was a college she had rarely needed to visit—she was seized with doubt. Was it wise to simply turn up? Would it upset him? What, after all, did Andrew really need?—and could she provide it?

These doors opened on further questions. Though she perceived, sharply, the necessity of action, its closer contours were shrouded in the fog of her own intentions. The pictures at the bop had surely needed destroying, as agents of Andrew's humiliation; but beyond that, what precisely had impelled her to hurtle over here? Why the drive, so intense, to *talk it over*? Was that really about righting a wrong, or was some part of her acting out of a scab-picking relish, a desire to dig into her own past? Her ears burned in remembrance of the looks she'd received at Christ's. Wasn't this just another version of the same sordid busybody impulse that she abhorred in everybody else?

Without the whetstone of oppositional argument, her nerve began to fail. Who was she to Andrew? He had never told her about this boy in the picture, or indeed any others. Had there been others? How many? And when? She felt ashamed. How swiftly these nosy questions came! What right had she to be told anything? But there was, beneath her own awful smallness, she thought, a genuine problem. If she mistrusted her own purposes, then so, quite fairly, might Andrew. It was entirely possible that she would be a bad, or at least a charged, presence, no matter however inoffensively she conducted herself. She had no concept of how he might react.

She leaned against the external college wall for a moment, but pulled away quickly as it sent icy fingers through her coat. This faffing about in the dark was doing no one any good. At last she took herself into the musty yellow warmth of the porter's lodge, silent save for the low tick-tick-tick of an old wooden clock, and deposited a hastily scribbled note in the pigeonhole marked TEO, A.C.S.:

*Andrew, I heard what happened at the bop. Really pissed off someone did that to you. Hope you're OK. If you want to talk about anything, let me know. You can call me anytime. Take care, Hwee Leng.*

It occurred to her, when she was midway through writing this, that the words of sympathy ought perhaps to have come before her own anger; but she sensed the danger, once she started on a search for the perfect text, of standing there all night. Better to just get it down and go. Leaving a note was that most feeble and hated of things—a compromise—but if she could neither abandon Andrew nor barge in on him unasked, she couldn't think what else to do.

She had the sensation, all through the windy uphill walk, that her mind was abuzz; but she had nothing to show for it as she unlocked her door and kicked her shoes to one corner of the scuffed and familiar carpet. Neither insight nor decision had struck. The business was both unfinished and futile. She retrieved her telephone book and sat for a long time on her bed, receiver in hand, staring at the accusing LED glow of her alarm clock. All the arguments against visiting applied with as much force to a call. In any case, it was much too late now; he was surely asleep. And yet. And yet. How could she just leave him, alone? Maybe he wasn't alone—he might have found comfort elsewhere—this mystery boy perhaps?—she hoped he had—but what if he hadn't? The unsteady carousel of her thoughts dizzied her. After an age, she began to dial, hesitated on the last digit, thought better of it, put the phone down, and went to bed. Against her expectations she slipped straight into a heavy black sleep. She only remembered to look at her email in the morning.

They'd found him by then. The misfortune of discovery fell to Rosie Warner, one of the army of women employed by the college to empty bins and change bedsheets. (Cambridge students were mysteriously assumed to be unable to carry out these tasks, or unwilling, or both.) Rosie spotted Andrew's slumped figure once she opened the door, and she rushed to free his body from the chokehold of cloth, but it was immediately obvious from his chill blue flesh that he had been dead for a while. Still she undid the knot around his throat before reconnecting the phone (someone had unplugged it at the wall) and ringing the porters for a doctor.

> **From: Chua Hwee Leng** <therealhweeleng@hotmail.com>
> **To:** Brian Teo <brianteo192@hotmail.com>
> **Date:** Thursday, 5 March 1998
> **Subject:** Fw: Check out the Pervert Scholar
> **Attachment:** Pervert.JPG

Brian, I'm so sorry about Andrew. I can't imagine how you and your parents are feeling.

I tried to ring you but no one picked up. I'll try again later, but in the meantime I thought I should send this to you anyway. There isn't going to be any good time to see it, and I don't think there is anything I can say to make it less horrible, but it's not fair for you not to know. I have more to tell you, but the basic story is: nobody admits to knowing who did this, and I don't know who the other guy in the picture is. I asked some of Andrew's neighbours and his college friends, but nobody has any idea. Whoever he is, I hope he's okay.

I deleted a bunch of email addresses from the message below, but this went to the scholarship mailing list, the scholarship officers at the CSB, and some other SingSoc people here.

I'm really sorry about everything. You take care ok? I'm thinking of you, and I'll call you soon.

Hwee Leng

Forwarded message begins:

**From: Pervert Scholar**
<singaporespervertscholar@hotmail.com>
**To:**
**Cc:**
**Date:** Tuesday, 3 March 1998
**Subject:** Check out the Pervert Scholar
**Attachment:** Pervert.JPG

> Check out this pervert scholar! What a disgusting pervert.
>
> Forwarded message ends.

Brian and Hwee Leng disagreed on the subject of investigation. The local coroner opened an inquest, as she did in all apparent cases of violent death, including suicide: but though the process would not produce a final report for months, the answers to the plain questions within its remit were never in doubt. It was Andrew who had died; he had died in his room in college; he had died shortly before daybreak; he had hanged himself. This much was all too well established.

There was no reason to expect more. After preliminary inquiries, the police quickly disclaimed interest: whatever else sending insulting emails or distributing embarrassing photographs might constitute, absent evidence of blackmail, they were not crimes under the law. College and the University made mournful noises, and then shrugged. It was sad, but sometimes people just couldn't handle stress. They dutifully reminded students and staff that in times of distress a counsellor was available on request.

That left the Singapore Civil Service Board, who was then not favourably disposed to Andrew. Government scholarships had been rocked by scandal lately, thanks to media reports of rogue scholars fleeing their obligations to service. These reprobates had to repay all monies received under their awards—no small sum even before you added a hefty rate of compound interest—so this was possible only for the tiniest minority. Nevertheless the Board was battling the perception that it existed to throw taxpayer money at privileged ingrates; and it did not welcome the further revelation that its ultra-selective processes had lavished resources upon someone so deplorably weak as to kill himself. And it could only be weakness. Everyone suffered, after all—every man had endured Basic Military Training—and it wasn't as if this generation of youngsters, who took for granted piped water and colour television and three square meals in their bellies each day, had ever known anything but coddled luxury. What could a Cambridge graduate reasonably complain about? Everyone suffered. Only the weak opted out.

No—the Board had its plate full. It couldn't control the electronic rumour mills, then still in toothless infancy, but it could prevent Andrew's sexual deviance from surfacing in the mainstream media. He had unsuspected emotional instabilities, aggravated by murky private disputes: that was the story, and though it was poor, as far as the public was concerned, it would have to be enough. The Board would not concern itself with the provenance of this unpleasant photograph, a question that could only return inconvenient answers. "Look at who got the email," Hwee Leng pointed out. "It's probably another scholar."

Perhaps Andrew's parents could have rolled the stiff wheels of one or more of these bureaucracies uphill. But they said nothing. What good would probing do? No doubt, from the email Brian had shown them, someone had been unkind; but at bottom this unkindness was only that of the universe, responding inexorably and impartially to something which did not fit. The identity or motivations of its anonymous agent did not matter: if not now, if not in this way, the disaster would have found another time to emerge, in some other form. Their son was a pervert, his death was a logical outgrowth of his warped nature, and his life had been a lie. They had failed him and themselves. They did not say any of this explicitly, but they didn't need to. After so many years, Brian knew it as if by osmosis. When he tried to tell them about the events at the bop, his father simply left the living room. His mother listened in silence and asked no questions.

"This kind of shameful thing," she said at last, in a broken voice. "Better not to talk about it."

"Hwee Leng told me," he said. "So I thought better tell you and Pa."

"Yah, it's good that you tell your parents," she said automatically. "But better not to talk to outsiders about this kind of shameful thing. I think better don't talk to this girl too much also." This direction astounded Brian: and perhaps some of his confusion showed in his face, because his mother went on, hesitantly, "Sometimes your mother thinks in a way it's also good that you didn't get a scholarship to go overseas and encounter all these bad influences. Singapore university also quite good, and at least you are at home with—the right kind of people, the right values."

Brian met her red and fearful gaze, and understood. She wanted him to reassure her. *Don't worry, Mum, I am not like Andrew.* Magic words that should be so easy to say. They were true enough in the sense that mattered to her—Brian only fancied girls—and once spoken they would lift some of that strain from her shoulders. But he couldn't do it. It wasn't fair to his brother that his mother should take comfort from such a thing. He didn't know what that fairness was worth, with Andrew dead, and his mother breathing, suffering, still. But Brian thought he understood Hwee Leng and her everyday state of anger better now: it ate at him that nobody else cared about what was fair to his brother. He looked away as the uneasy mix of hope and anxiety in his mother's face drained into a kind of doubtful misery, and she left him on the sofa without a further word.

Then he felt sick at heart: he had done her a deliberate injury. Some lizard brain reflex rose in reproach: who was he to sit in judgment of his mother, who had given him everything? But the feeling slithered away as soon as it came, because the response, for once, was clear. He was Andrew's brother.

Still, Brian was no more inclined than his parents to

pursue the details of who had done what to whom. What they saw as shameful he simply found futile.

"There's just no point."

"But there's a real person behind this," Hwee Leng said. "Or people—maybe more than one. They shouldn't just *get away with it*."

But how could they be unmasked? There was barely any evidence to go on, even with the suspects narrowed down to the Singaporean students at Cambridge. Andrew had left no hints: his computer hard drive was blank, his college pigeonhole empty except for a bank statement and Hwee Leng's forlorn note, apparently unread. In theory, the sender of the email might be traced through an IP address, but without legal compulsion the company that administered the account would surely never divulge that information. Probably nothing could have been gleaned from the hard copies of the photograph, pawed over by just about everyone at the bop, even if they hadn't been mostly reduced by Hwee Leng to sodden bits of trash. And while the young man pictured might have furnished a clue as to how anyone else had come by the shot, his identity remained an enigma.

"I bet you the CSB could find out," Hwee Leng said. "If they kept digging and put some pressure on. Someone would crack eventually. They should at least try. Aren't they concerned about having such a malicious scholar in their ranks?"

"What can they do about it?"

"I don't know. Some professional downgrading, maybe, in their postings or something, when they come back. You know they keep files on everyone. They rate and rank all their people. But even if not, don't you think it matters to *know*? Don't you want to find out just what the hell went on?"

Brian wasn't so sure. He shared, he thought, Hwee Leng's basic sentiment: that even if it was of no practical consequence—no one punished, no acts reversed—it was better to understand than not. What he doubted, though he didn't know how to explain it, was that any of the forensic detail that she so craved would help him understand any better.

Suppose Brian had names and dates and faces for all of it: the boy in the picture, when it was taken, how someone got hold of it, who they were, where they made the copies, what they were doing now. These things, he felt, could alter none of the fundamentals. They could neither soften the terrible knowledge he had gained, nor lessen the terrible ignorance against which he stumbled. The essential facts had long been to hand—the tyrannical possibility of such petty cruelty, the wonder and the strangeness of his brother, and the unfathomable bitterness of that brother's despair—and he grasped as much of them as he ever would. No one would ever be able to tell him what he most wanted to learn: what Andrew had hoped for all these years, and how Brian could have helped.

# EPILOGUE

Sunlight is a different creature here, a buttery gold, softening stone, soaking wood, seeping into green leaf to give off a rich fat sheen. He has often thought how odd it is that a country that receives so little sunshine should be so perfected by it.

A narrow slab of warmth is falling across his bed through a gap in the curtains. Outside, treetops gently wave. He shifts and turns to lay a cheek against the cool pillowcase. The sheets are fresh against his legs. Clean cloth on skin. This, his favourite season, always surprises him with how beautiful it is. At first, he supposed this was because it was all new to him; but he has since learned that spring is always new, that is the whole point of it. This is his fourth now, and it is still new.

He could lie here forever, he thinks. This is all he needs. But there is so much to look forward to doing, and to do it he must break up his present contentment. This is a good problem to have.

After a few moments he pulls himself up and sits, leaning back on his pillow, propped against the wall. Still tucked up snug to his hips under the cheap green duvet. The picture is lying on the bedside stand and he can't keep from the indulgence of picking it up, or smiling as he studies himself next to those dark curls and that fey, mobile face. The scene is from shortly before he persuaded Graham—and not just with words—to put the camera aside. His penis stirs lazily at the memory. It was a distraction at the time, but he is glad of the photograph now. It will be a charm against the corrosions of memory, against unreality. He turns it over. On the back a phone number is set out in large, round digits, in black felt pen. *Edinburgh*, it says below that. *Come say hello. G x.*

Will he ever make it up there, to Scotland? He doesn't know. He has no particular plans to do so, but it is possible. Many things seem possible to him this morning. He has been led into bed, easily, pleasurably, repeatedly, by a visiting researcher, after a commonplace drink in the college bar. It was very simple. He feels sorry for his younger self. (And enjoys it. Pity is a lofty feeling.) His old agonies had such a cosmic scale. But sex, it turns out, is a practical problem with a practical solution.

He can't really blame himself, though, for having seen no other option than furious and total celibacy, of the mind as well as body. There have always seemed to him to be unbreakable binds, promises to keep, cause and effect; if you move part A in one direction, the physical logic of joints requires a predetermined result of part B. If you want to be safe, you have to play, absolutely, by the rules. He stretches in the late morning light. He isn't giving up this view at all—he understands the need for caution—he just sees, now, that there are moments of flex, room for secrets, spaces to work it out. He sees that while you cannot escape the bargain, you can cheat it, around the edges. You can game the system. He knows this is greedy. But greed seems, after Graham, suddenly vital. That is the gift this time is making to him. He will take this picture with him when he leaves, to remind himself of the future's hidey-hole openings, of all the possibilities waiting for him if he only keeps himself alive to them. He stares out at the intense blue of the sky, this blue that is almost a thing he can hold.

There is a rap on the door and a "Hey!" The day is calling.

"Hold on a sec!" He thrusts the photograph under his pillow, pulls on a T-shirt, and goes to answer. "Hey."

"Come on leh, Sleeping Beauty, we have to get the drinks and stuff for tonight."

"Sure. I got to do my teeth, give me a few minutes."

"Yah, yah. Just don't take all day."

He yanks some clothes from his chest of drawers and makes his way along the few metres of corridor to the bathroom. He isn't away for very long. Just long enough for his visitor to perch, waiting, among the mussed layers of the duvet. To notice the square slip of paper that has fallen to the floor. To pick it up, study it, and slip it quietly into the back pocket of his jeans.

Just long enough for the last brittle thread of an old admiration to snap, betrayed.

Nothing seems out of place as he returns, his face washed, his hair brushed, ready and smiling.

"I'm done," he says. "Let's go."

# ACKNOWLEDGEMENTS

Thank you to everyone at Epigram Books who has worked so hard to bring *A Certain Exposure* into the world—especially my patient and supportive editor, Jason Erik Lundberg.

This novel has benefited hugely from the time and energy of its early readers: Jack Anderson, Dave Anthony, Sarah Howe, Jane Pek, Tim Saunders and Wong Pei Chi. Special mention must go to the Heidelberg Writers Group—*vielen Dank*!

Yu-Mei Balasingamchow, Li Wenying and Pooja Makhijani helped me to navigate the world of publishing; Michelle Tan and Esther Tan provided insight into medical procedures; the National Environment Agency answered a query about weather records; Vincent Cheng wrote an important account of detention without trial; and the Internet's collective wisdom resolved numerous points of fact. Errors are mine alone.

Most of all, thank you to Tim, for the love that makes everything else possible, and to Iris, for joy.

# ABOUT THE AUTHOR

Jolene Tan studied at Cambridge University and Harvard Law School, and currently works at AWARE, Singapore's leading gender equality advocacy group. *A Certain Exposure* is her first novel.